CHAMBA

THE CELESTIAL VALLEY

GOOD EARTH PUBLICATIONS
Eicher Goodearth Limited
New Delhi

Supported by
DEPARTMENT OF LANGUAGE AND CULTURE
GOVERNMENT OF HIMACHAL PRADESH

A GOOD EARTH PUBLICATION

Copyright © 2007 Eicher Goodearth Limited, New Delhi
ISBN 81-87780-41-X

Editor and Publisher: Swati Mitra
Senior Editor: Parvati Sharma

Designer: Baishakhee Sengupta
Editorial Team: Samia Sharma, Vaijyanti Ghose
Contributors: Damyanti Ghose: *Arts and Crafts*
Hari Chauhan: *Bhuri Singh Museum*
Vijay Sharma: *Painting in Chamba*

Photographs:
Hari Chauhan 62Above&Below; Rajesh Singh Charak 6, 82-85;
Vijay Sharma 86-91; Parvati Sharma 5, 8A, 11, 14A, 19, 20Centre, 21-22, 26B, 27,
32-37, 38B, 39, 41-43, 44B Left, 44B Right, 46, 49C, 50A, 51, 54-55, 56A&B, 57,
59B, 61A, 62C, 63, 64A, 66B, 67B, 68A, 69B, 71, 73, 74B, 75-77, 81A, 96, 97B,
108; Swati Mitra 4, 8B, 10, 13, 15-16, 23-24, 26A, 28-31, 38A, 40, 44A&C, 48,
49B, 50B, 52A&C, 53A, 56C, 58, 59A, 60, 62Background, 64B, 66A, 68B, 69A,
70, 78B, 79C&B, 94B, 95, 105-107, Cover

Maps:
Advisor: Lt. Gen. (Retd.) S. M. Chadha
Design: Madhumita Rao

The photographs on the following pages have been used
with the kind permission of:
Bhuri Singh Museum, Chamba 14B, 52B, 53B, 61B, 94A, 98-101
Department of Language and Culture, Shimla 7, 12, 18, 20A, 20B
Government Museum and Art Gallery, Chandigarh 72, 92-93
Himachal Pradesh Tourism Development Corporation 80B
State Museum, Shimla 97A

Special thanks to Ashok Thakur, Principal Secretary,
Department of Language and Culture, Government of HP
Prem Sharma, Director, Department of Language and Culture
Prem Sharma, DLO, Chamba

CHAMBA

THE CELESTIAL VALLEY

HISTORY AND GEOGRAPHY

'The mountain region has been the abode of hermits, and the haunt of kings...' (S. L. Nagar, *The Temples of Himachal Pradesh*)

The valleys of Himachal Pradesh occupy a special place in India's history and geography. Dwarfed by magnificent snow-capped peaks, cut through by sparkling rivers, and dense with forests, the valleys have nurtured *rishis* and rajas, shepherds and weavers, goldsmiths and architects, through the rise and fall of Empires, religions and aesthetics across the Indian plains.

Two of these valleys, the Ravi and Pangi (formed by the Chandrabhaga river), are included in the district of Chamba in north-west Himachal Pradesh. Of these, the Ravi valley is more fertile, populated and pretty, 'presenting many delightful contrasts'. The Pangi valley, however, is more challenging, though it rewards the intrepid with views of a divine imagination. The *Gazetteer of the Chamba State* (1904) describes it as 'unique in its grandeur and beauty... The scenery is sublime and imposing, and Nature appears in her wildest and grandest moods'.

⌃ Above: Serene mountain views of Chamba

◄ Left: Painstakingly terraced fields light up the landscape

▶ Right: In the celestial valley, a roadside Shiva in worship

In the higher passes, 'no sound disturbs the stillness, except that of falling rock…. The coolies even are silent… for Bhagwati, the presiding deity, disapproves of any noise within her domain'. And when, finally, the 'summit is gained… a panorama, in its beauty and grandeur far surpassing any possible conception, lies before' (*Gazetteer of the Chamba State*, 1904).

The journey into Pangi was once so fraught with danger that state officials would get a special 'funeral' allowance when they travelled here, and even today it remains inaccessible for much of the year.

All of Chamba, in fact, including the lower valleys, is relatively isolated, and this particular feature of its history has made Chamba something of a 'sanctuary' of antiquity, 'invaluable to the student of India's ancient history' (*Gazetteer*). In particular, Chamba is famous for its wood and stone temples, such as Lakshmi-Narayana, Radha-Krishna, Hari Rai, Lakshana Devi and Shakti Devi, many beautifully carved, most with decorations and sculptures intact.

▼ Below: Pangi's forbidding snow begins to melt with the approach of summer

▲ Above: The old Sitla bridge, once the only the only entry to Chamba town, now replaced by a modern construction

Other architectural features of the region include bridges (especially the attractive though precarious *jhoola*, or swing bridges, strung across the Ravi's deep waters), and 'fountain stones', once placed near springs, now in museums. Often elaborately carved and dedicated to Varuna, the god of water, rivers and oceans, or erected in memory of the dead, many of these fountain stones are dated – thus providing invaluable clues to historians.

A majority of these stones were erected by local feudatory chiefs, the Thakurs and Ranas who ruled the region until, over the centuries, an unbroken line of Chamba Rajas consolidated their power, while the chieftains were either assimilated into the government, or returned to their primary occupation, agriculture.

The Chamba Rajas claimed descent from the Suryavanshi line of Rajputs, and Vishnu heads their genealogical rolls, with Rama appearing down on the list at 63rd. The first historical figure is Maru, who is said to have battled the chieftains of the upper Ravi valley and founded Bharmour, Chamba's first capital, sometime in the mid 6th century AD. Thereafter, he gave the new kingdom to his youngest son, and retired to a life of asceticism.

⌃ Above: Rock inscriptions such as this are treasures for historians

⌄ Below: The Pir Panjal

Over the next century or so, Bharmour prospered and gained a respected place amongst neighbouring kingdoms. The chronicles of Kullu, for example, record that a Raja of Bharmour participated in conferences with the rulers of Ladakh, Bushahr, Kangra etc.

These chronicles further record that in the late 7th century, Bharmour waged a successful war on Kullu, under Meru Varman, who extended the kingdom's boundaries almost as far as its future capital. He is also credited with building the temples of Manimahesh, Lakshana Devi and Ganesh among others.

Under Lakshmi Varman, who ruled *c.* 800 AD, a severe epidemic devastated the kingdom. Drawn by its weakness, tribes from the higher mountains, possibly Tibet, charged down. The Raja was killed, and Kullu asserted its independence. His pregnant wife fled to Kangra, giving birth on the way to her son, in a cave in the upper Ravi valley. Fearing for his life, she might have abandoned the baby had her companions not persuaded her otherwise; and when she returned to pick up the child, she found him surrounded by a crowd of protective mice. In recognition of this debt, the child was named Mushan and it became a tradition that mice caught in the Chamba palaces would not be killed.

Spread across an area of 6,528 sq kms, and ranging in height from 600 to 6,400 m, Chamba is divided into six sub-divisions, Bharmour, Bhattiyat, Chamba, Churah (Tissa), Dalhousie and Pangi. Of these, Dalhousie, Chamba and Bharmour form a line running southeast from the western tip of the Dhauladhar to the southern Pir Panjal. The remaining divisions are to the north, entering the progressively starker landscapes of the northern Pir Panjal and, beyond, the daunting Pangi range.

These three mountain ranges, ranging from verdant hills to forbidding peaks, enclose the region, cushioning it against outside invasions and influence in the past, and against the flood of tourists that characterises lower districts such as Kullu in the present.

Eventually, in the half-mythical, almost fairytale manner that characterises Chamba's history, Mushan Varman married the princess of Suket, gained an army and recovered his kingdom.

In *c.* 920 AD one of Chamba's best known rulers gained the throne. Sahila Varman, fifth in line after Mushan, waged a 12-year war on Kullu, is said to have conquered Kangra and even, perhaps, battled the armies of early Turkish invaders. He also extended his domain along the lower Ravi valley. In these campaigns, he was accompanied by his daughter, Champavati.

When passing through the land where the present capital stands, Champavati was captivated, and begged her father to shift his capital to these serene hills. Although Sahila Varman did not want to refuse, he was hesitant. The land was the livelihood of Brahmins. Eventually, a deal was negotiated, whereby all Brahmins would receive 8 copper coins whenever the town celebrated a marriage.

And so a new capital was established: Chamba.

Piety and an easy relationship with the mystical is characteristic not just of the Chamba dynasty but of the mountain populace. Perhaps an effect of their isolated surroundings, perhaps of the classical magnificence of their environment; the struggle to survive along rocky precipices, and the delight of living in a world of wildflowers and scented woods; or perhaps a combination of factors, this spirituality is inseparable from the history, and culture, of Chamba.

So it is said that Sahila Varman was promised 10 sons by 84 visiting sages. Perhaps pragmatically, the Raja invited the sages to stay in his kingdom until their prophecy came true. Many years later, when the new capital was established, Sahila Varman faced an acute water crisis. According to tradition, he dreamt that for water to flow to Chamba, he must sacrifice a son. But the queen, Sunanya, begged to be allowed to give her own life instead.

A grave procession was organised. The queen walked bareheaded, accompanied by handmaidens, and was buried alive. Water began flowing into town.

Sahila Varman made a shrine to his queen, popularly known as Sui Mata, where she stopped to rest, now the site of an annual fair, unique for never being interrupted, no matter what the cause.

Chamba	India
C. 550 AD	
Bharmour founded by legendary Maru.	End of Gupta dynasty.
C. 680 AD	
Bharmour's Meru Varman extends empire and builds Lakshana Devi and Shakti Devi temples.	
C. 800 AD	
Rule of Lakshmi Varman; plague and invasions weaken the kingdom.	Pratihara dynasty strengthens rule in Kannauj.
C. 920 AD	
Rule of Sahila Varman; new capital established at Chamba.	
C. 940 AD	
Rule of Yugakara Varman.	
C. 1040 AD	
Rule of Salavahana Varman; Kashmir invades hill-states.	Western Chalukyas rule north and north-west India.
C. 1120 AD	
Rule of Udaiya Varman; Kashmir weakened and Chamba regains independence.	Turks invade north Indian kingdoms.
C. 1175 AD	
Rule of Vijaya Varman; Chamba's boundaries extended.	Invasion of Mohammad Ghori.
C. 1526 AD	
	Foundation of Mughal dynasty
C. 1556 AD	
Rule of Pratap Singh Varman; Lakshmi-Narayana complex renovated.	Akbar crowned emperor; hill-states annexed.

The Raja also built the Champavati temple for his daughter, where too a fair is held every year.

The king reposed great faith in a particular sage, Charpatnath, for whom he built a temple, and in whose honour he struck the Chamba coin with the symbol of a *yogi*, a pierced ear. Most famously, however, Sahila Varman built the Lakshmi-Narayana shrine.

Sahila Varman wanted only the best marble for the image of Vishnu in the Laskhmi-Narayana temple, and he sent nine sons on a mission to the Vindhyas, to bring back a block. When the marble was carved, however, it was found unsuitable for the main image, and so it was used to make three smaller images of Shiva, Ganesha and Lakhsmi. The nine princes set out again, but this time, tragically, they were murdered by robbers on their return journey. Undaunted, Sahila Varman sent his youngest son, Yugakara, to retrieve the marble. Thus, finally and at great personal cost, the Raja had a grand Vishnu idol made.

Such tenacity of purpose ensured Sahila Varman a prominent space in Chamba's annals. In inscriptions dated to the early 11th century, he is described as one 'who had made the circuit of the seven worlds fragrant by his fame… by looking upon whose lovely presence the eyes of the world have been made fruitful' (*Gazetteer*).

⌄ Below: An old photograph of the Lakshmi-Narayana complex

▶ Right: The beautifully carved Vishnu in the Lakshmi-Narayana temple

Then, at the end of a successful, prosperous reign, Sahila Varman followed in the tradition of many Chamba Rajas including the founder of the dynasty, Maru, and retired to a life of asceticism and contemplation. His son, Yugakara, is best known for building the Gauri-Shankar temple in the Lakshmi-Narayana complex.

Another century passed. It was the dawn of Islamic incursions but also the height of many indigenous kingdoms. Among these was Kashmir, which invaded Chamba in the early decades of the 11th century. The Raja, Salavahana Varman was deposed, perhaps killed, and his sons enthroned as subjects of the Kashmiri state. It was only around 1120 AD, when Islamic armies had weakened Kashmir, that Chamba became independent again.

This development makes another peculiarity of Chamba's history apparent. Although it was relatively easy for rulers from the plains to subjugate the small state in times of peace, chaos would almost invariably spell freedom, and even prosperity, for the hills. So, for example, Vijaya Varman, ruling *c.* 1175 AD, took advantage of the Ghori invasions to attack Kashmir and Ladakh, enriching his kingdom and greatly extending its boundaries.

Chamba remained independent for over 400 years, while all around empires rose and fell. In the plains, the Mughals were gaining strength, but were not yet comfortable enough to attempt incursions into the hills beyond the Shivalik range. By the early 16th century though, it seemed likely that they would soon try. Perhaps this consideration prompted Ganesha Varman, who ruled *c.* 1512 AD, to build the Ganeshgarh fort, to protect his frontier south of the Dhauladhar range.

His apprehension proved correct. In 1556, Akbar was crowned emperor, and one of his first acts was to strike the Kangra fort. Chamba remained undisturbed a few more years, though, and Ganesha Varman's successor, Pratap Singh Varman (*c.* 1559 AD) managed to devote some time to repairing the Lakshmi-Narayana temple, and even extended his boundaries to Guler.

⌃ Above: Mountain settlements, the fruit of centuries of effort

⌃ Above left: Detail from the Chamunda Devi temple, which may be even older than Lakshmi-Narayana

◀ Left: Detail from a fountain stone, found across Chamba, but especially in Pangi

It was not long before Chamba surrendered to Akbar. Though subject to Mughal rule, the hill kingdoms managed to retain a great degree of autonomy. No longer allowed the honorific 'Raja' and required to pay annual tributes, the rulers, at the same time, were given lavish gifts and appointed to fairly high offices in the Mughal court and armies.

It was not uncommon for the hill kingdoms to war with each other, and appeal to the Mughal emperor for aid in the form of men and arms. Often enough, the appeal was granted.

So it was that Jagat Singh of Nurpur attacked Janardan of Chamba in a war that lasted 12 years, until Jagat Singh enlisted Jehangir's aid, and Janardan surrendered. At the meeting called to discuss peace, the treacherous Jagat Singh stabbed and murdered Janardan, who could not retaliate because his dagger was tied to its sheath. Ever since, the kings of Chamba have worn their daggers loose.

▼ Below: A village on the banks of the Ravi

Chamba's two great rivers, the Ravi and the Chandrabhaga, are responsible for much of its fabled beauty.

The Ravi enters Chamba from the Pir Panjal to the east and flows northwest, collecting numerous tributaries on the way. Of these the most significant are the Budhil, which meets the Ravi a few kilometres west of Bharmour, and the Siul, its largest tributary, which joins the river past Chamba town. At the district's western border, the river turns south, flowing into Punjab.

The Ravi's waters, sometimes collected into serene blue lagoons by a series of dams, sometimes flowing fast and free, water the fields of southern Chamba, giving this region its fertile and fragrant landscape.

The Chandrabhaga, by contrast, is a more challenging river, rising in the heights of Lahaul-Spiti and flowing through the desolate Pangi mountains. In this region it is also known as the Chenab.

Janardan's son, Prithvi Singh, escaped to Mandi, waiting to reclaim his kingdom. Jagat Singh was now well established in Chamba: he had built the Taragarh fort, now in ruins, and distinguished himself in service to Jehangir and Shahjehan. He seemed invulnerable until, in 1641, Jagat Singh made a fatal miscalculation. He rebelled.

Immediately, Shahjehan sent his son Murad Baksh with an army to subdue the rebellion. Prithvi Singh acted quickly. Gathering together an army borrowed from the rulers of Mandi and Suket, the prince marched through the dangerous passes of Lahaul and Pangi to reach Chamba and assist the Mughal army.

His aid was appreciated, and the *Badshanama* records that: '…the highborn prince [Murad Baksh], in accordance with the sublime orders, sent Prithvi Chand, the Zamindar of Champa… to the royal household, the abode of great kings…. [He] was honoured with a *khilat*, an inlaid dagger, the title of 'Commander of one thousand', and the actual command of 400 horsemen, the title of Raja and a horse…' (*Gazetteer*).

Meanwhile Jagat Singh and his son were captured and brought to the Darbar 'with halters round their necks'. It is perhaps indicative of the affection, and faith, that the Mughals reposed in their hill feudatories that Jagat Singh was pardoned, and even granted all his previous honours.

Chamba was restored to its dynasty. Prithvi Singh even expanded his territory, building state offices in Pangi; and became something of a favourite in Shahjehan's court, from whom he received many gifts, including jewellery and a *jagir* of Rs. 26,000. The greatest honour, however, was accorded him by the women of the emperor's *zenana* who, hearing of Prithvi Singh's good looks, begged to see him. So, he was led through the women's quarters blindfolded, much to their delight.

Several temples were built during his reign, including the Nag temple at Khajjiar and Sita-Rama at Chamba.

Several decades of peace and prosperity followed, and when Udai Singh gained the throne in 1690 AD there was little sense of foreboding. Unfortunately, Udai Singh was more frivolous than his predecessors, and court officials grew increasingly disturbed by his misrule.

Eventually, when the king appointed a barber as Wazir because he had fallen in love with his daughter, the officials hatched a plot to assassinate him. They enlisted the support of Lakshman Singh, the king's brother.

In a touching (and in the annals of power, uncommon) vindication of blood over water, on the day of the assassination Lakshman Singh was so moved by his brother's appeals that he changed sides, and was himself killed alongside the king.

The double-assassination occurred in Udaipur, some 10 kms from Chamba. The successor, Uggar Singh, was haunted by his cousin's ghost and so built a small shrine here, and the scene of the assassination remains uncultivated to this day.

But blood had been shed, and Chamba now witnessed a period of internecine warfare. Uggar Singh was deposed in favour of another cousin, Dalel Singh. It is said that Uggar Singh watched his approach from the Chamunda temple, perched high above Chamba town, before fleeing to Kangra. Then, in 1748 Uggar Singh's son claimed the throne. Unpredictably, Dalel Singh chose to recognise the claim, and handed over the kingdom, retiring as an ascetic to Jwalamukhi.

⌄ Below, left and right: Chamba, then and now. In both the royal palace is visible

Despite the generosity of this gesture, the Chamba kings might have had to suspend hostilities. As Mughal rule began to disintegrate, as Marathas and Afghans launched a 'life-and-death struggle for the mastery of India', and the Sikhs emerged as a significant power, the hill kingdoms had to be swift, nimble and united to survive.

So, in 1775 AD, Raja Raj Singh paid Rs. 1 lakh to an army of Ramgarhia Sikhs who helped him fight Jammu's incursions into Chamba. This was barely achieved when Kangra attacked. Through misfortune, Raj Singh found himself with only 45 men confronting the Kangra army. Heroically, he chose to fight, with prayers and gratitude, it is said, to Chamunda Devi, goddess of war.

▲ Above: Lord Dalhousie

Kangra grew ever stronger and its king, Sansar Chand, impelled by hubris, annexed more and more territory until the other hill kingdoms joined to suppress him. Under siege in Kangra fort, he appealed to Ranjit Singh, who came to his aid but also made him a feudatory.

Chamba too might have suffered a similar fate but, as always, its topography was its greatest strength. Additionally, a powerful court official called Nathu cultivated a friendship with the Sikh Maharaja, buying his state many years of respite.

▲ Top: The bazaar at Chamba

▼ Below: Post office of Chamba

Wazir Nathu's death was perhaps as much a blow to Chamba as Ranjit Singh's was to Punjab. And, after a period of chaos and bloodshed, both fell to the British.

▶ Right: Modern Chamba

And so Chamba became part of colonised India. Soon, the rule of princes and Rajas would end. Modern construction would make its forest and valleys more accessible, and modern transport would entail greater communication between the spiritual innocence of the mountains and the more pragmatic plains. A Sanatorium would be built, Dalhousie, and become a cherished retreat across India. Finally, Chamba would be open, a gift of beauty to all visitors.

And yet, its myths and legends, its many histories of *sadhus* and kings, miracles and sacrifice remain half-hidden from the grander narratives of Empire. For those who make the journey, however, these stories are as enchanting as the valleys in which they occurred.

TEMPLE ARCHITECTURE

Most scholars agree that there are at least three distinct styles of temple architecture evident in Himachal Pradesh. These are commonly referred to as Nagara, or *shikhara* style, the pentroof and the pagoda. Of these, the last does not appear in Chamba at all, while stone *shikhara* shrines begin appearing only after the 10th century AD. Chamba's 'original' architecture, therefore, is the wooden pentroof.

▲ Above and right: Chamba's two temple styles as exemplified by Lakshana Devi and the Lakshmi-Narayana complex

It is difficult, however, to make any definite pronouncements about temple styles in these remote regions. In the *District Gazetteer*, for example, it is speculated that the Shakti Devi shrine at Chhatrari may have had a pagoda roof. Later, since climatic conditions in the hills necessitated frequent renovations of temple roofs, the temple may have acquired its present shape (*Gazetteer of the Chamba State*, 1904).

It is quite remarkable, in fact, that any of the original structure of these 1,000 year old temples survives, and a great deal of the credit goes to the strong deodar, or cedar, wood used in their construction.

For the lay reader, the *Gazetteer* provides a handy nomenclature for Chamba's temples, distinguishing them as Plains and Hill types. The Plains type follows the conventions of Nagara temples, though on a smaller scale and with some alterations (for example the circular projection just below the temple's peak, intended to protect its walls from rain and snow) to suit local topography and climate; is built of stone; and is profusely carved on the outside.

Hill type shrines, on the other hand, are elaborately carved, and often painted, on the inside. The *Gazetteer* describes the usual pattern thus: 'Their construction is remarkably simple. They consist of a small cella [*garbhagriha*], usually raised on a square plinth, and built of layers of rubble masonry alternating with beams of cedar wood. This is surmounted by a sloping roof of slates or wooden shingles supported by wooden posts, which form a veranda or procession path round the shrine.... Though simple in their architecture, some of these Hill temples are of great interest owing to the elaborate decoration of their façades, ceilings and pillars'.

Most temples, whatever the style of their construction, have a compound, in which there is an image of the main deity's mount – Shiva temples, for example, have a Nandi facing them, Devi shrines have colourfully painted tigers at the gates and doorways, and shrines dedicated to Vishnu often have images of Garuda, raised on a pole, the Garuda *stambha*.

Another characteristic of these temples is the profusion of bells, both big and small, strung up at the entrance and, if the temple has a veranda, along its walls.

Finally, most temples are marked with a triangular, brightly coloured flag. Often these are visible from a great distance, announcing the presence of the divine in this most secluded of landscapes.

THE EVOLUTION OF INDIAN TEMPLES

Though some scholars have written that Chamba's wooden temples evolved into quite unique forms of architectural expression, possibly derived from Kashmir, the stone *shikhara* shrines are part of a well-defined, north Indian style, called Nagara.

Initially built exclusively around a *garbhagriha*, the core sanctum, stone temples expanded greatly as more and more ritual began to form part of regular worship.

The *mandapa*, for example, evolved as a place for congregation. In this way, many elaborate structures were built in the plains.

In the hills, however, the lack of large expanses of flat land has meant that *shikhara* shrines do not usually have grand assembly halls; while wooden temples usually have a verandah around the *garbhagriha* for the purpose.

FROM BHARMOUR TO CHAMBA

At an altitude of 2,130 m, approximately 70 kms from Chamba town, Bharmour was the first capital of this region, founded in the 6th century AD by Maru. This legendary ruler and sage was not indigenous to these parts, but is said to have travelled here from Ayodhya.

⌃ Above: Bharmour's charming Chaurasi complex

To complicate matters, some scholars have even speculated on the location of Bharmour. Originally, the settlement was called Brahmapura, a name which could be used to denote 'any town where Brahmins were settled'. So, it has been suggested, Bharmour may in fact have had its genesis as a 'moving royal camp, where also Brahmins attached to the king were living' (Hermann Goetz, *The Early Wooden Temples of Chamba*, 1955).

Whatever the historical facts, by the late 7th century, Bharmour was well established as the capital of the region's Gurjara-supported rulers.

Set in a valley formed by the Budhil, a tributary of the Ravi, Bharmour was and continues to be extremely picturesque. For modern visitors 'the wide Budhil valley… resembles the most beautiful parts of Switzerland. Its people, the Gaddi shepherds and cowherds, their wooden houses with balconies like Swiss chalets, their milk production complemented by… millet fields, vegetable gardens and bee keeping, likewise create an illusion of Switzerland' (Hermann Goetz).

The three hour drive from Chamba town to Bharmour can easily stretch to five – travellers may want to stop at a number of places to admire the compelling views. The gurgling river flows alongside, sometimes passing under wooden swing bridges, sometimes collected into the lakes formed by small-scale dam projects (Chamera 2 and 3). The hills are painstakingly carved into terraced fields, and dotted with settlements. Bridle paths twist up the hillsides, and waterfalls gush down.

About 28 kms from Chamba town is a shrine to **Tirlochan Mahadev**, comprising a rock on the river bed with a large statue of Shiva. The rock is, supposedly, the body of Tirlochan, a devout

◀ Left: Views along the road to Bharmour

▼ Below left: The Tirlochan Mahadev shrine

bhakta of Shiva. A tailor by profession, Tirlochan found himself in Shiva's presence when swimming in the Manimahesh lake. The god asked the tailor to make him some clothes, and Tirlochan spent several months in this service. On his return, Shiva gave him a sackful of wool, and cautioned him never to reveal the secret of his disappearance.

Back home, Tirlochan tried resisting his wife's inquiries, but eventually succumbed. As the words left his mouth, the tailor lost his mind. He ran senseless from the house and took a suicidal leap into the Ravi's fierce waters, from which his body washed up as a rock. Meanwhile, the sack of wool opened to reveal gold.

▲ Above: A sign on the road from Khadamukh marks the first view of the Manimahesh peak

▲ Above right: The sacred mountain itself, still far away

As the road climbs higher, it narrows and its condition deteriorates, perhaps the only drawback of the journey. A little under 15 kms from Bharmour, at **Khadamukh**, there is a confluence of the Budhil with the Ravi, and from here on the Budhil valley begins.

The mountains are more stark here, the air much cooler. A kilometre further, the Manimahesh peak comes into view, gleaming in the distance. Another half an hour, and the road reaches Bharmour, a fresh, clean town, so ancient it is almost timeless.

Over 1,300 years ago, Bharmour's natural beauty was considerably enhanced by Meru Varman (*c.* 680 AD), Bharmour's most renowned king, both a great warrior and possessed of a fine aesthetic style. As patron of the fabulously talented sculptor, Gugga, the king built some of the district's fascinating wooden temples. Of these, the Lakshana Devi, Ganesh and Manimahesh temples are in Bharmour, and Shakti Devi in Chhatrari, a few kilometres along the road to Chamba.

▲ Above: The stunning image of Lakshana Devi, her eyes inlaid with silver

TEMPLES IN BHARMOUR: THE CHAURASI AND BRAHMANI DEVI

The Bharmour temples are located within the Chaurasi (Eighty-four) complex for which the town is known. The complex may have some connection with the 84 wise men who, reputedly, advised the 10th century ruler Sahila Varman.

Today, Chaurasi approximates as a town square – a place where children play while their parents stroll and chat, a place to sit and watch the world go by.

Gugga, who sculpted the Lakshana Devi and Ganesh deities here, was among those 'artists who were not only expected to be well versed in the respective professional skills, but were also supposed to possess sufficient knowledge of the religious texts for translating their skills into practice' (S. L. Nagar, *The Temples of Himachal Pradesh*, 1990).

△ Top left and right: Children play among the gods at Chaurasi

△ Above: High mountains shelter the complex

Among the 'professional skills' that good artists were expected to have, as listed in the *Samarangana Sutradhara*, were intuition, close observation, technical skill, knowledge of measurements, balance and anatomy, the ability to depict moods, intelligence and self-control.

29

That Gugga possessed these qualities and more
is obvious from even a photograph of the idols.
Lakshana Devi, for example, perfectly conveys
both grace and strength, femininity and divinity.
The slim-waisted goddess stands effortlessly
on the buffalo demon's head, piercing his neck
with her trident – perhaps a symbol of lightning
– yet radiating not anger but a sanctified beauty.
Her eyes are inlaid with silver, her hair bound
in pearls; fine muslin falls below her waist, and
she wears exquisite armlets, anklets and other
jewellery. Besides the trident, she is armed with
a sword; while a third hand is in the act of lifting
the demon off the ground.

Standing slightly over 90 cms in height, the image
is inscribed thus: 'Aum. This image of Lakshana
Devi, for the increase of his own virtue, was
dedicated by Meru Varman Deva, the son of Sri
Divakara Varman Deva, the grandson of Sri Bala
Varman Deva, the great-grandson of Sri Aditya
Varman Deva, of the race of Mohsunaswa, and
family of Aditya. Made by Gugga' (S. L. Nagar).

Modern convention, however, dictates that this
and other sculptures are covered in silken fabric
and jewellery.

▲ Above: Details from
the temple's walls and
pillars

The temple itself is wooden, in the pentroof style. Some of its carvings, especially along the façade, have faded under the assault of 'the snow and rain of 13 centuries' (S. L. Nagar). Inside, however, especially on the ceiling, many details remain, including fantastic animal figures and geometric motifs.

⌃ Above: The imposing Manimahesh temple

The **Manimahesh temple** has a *linga* as its main deity. This stone temple may be older than the bronze Nandi that stands facing it, and an inscription on the marble inside dates the building to the 15th century.

The figures of Ganga and Yamuna at the entrance also hint at a later construction – their traditional mounts, the crocodile and tortoise, have transmuted into birds.

31

The 1.5 m high **Nandi**, however, has an inscription that ascribes both the temple and the bull to Meru Varman's patronage: before the temple '[was set the bull, fat of cheeks and body, compact of breast and hump, the exalted vehicle of god Shiva]. This is the glorious work of the illustrious Meru Varman [famous] over four oceans, [tending] continually to increase the [spiritual] fruits of his parents and himself. Made by the workman Gugga' (S. L. Nagar).

It is conjectured therefore that the Manimahesh temple was extensively rebuilt by one of Meru Varman's successors.

The shrine displays a peculiarity of hill architecture – the top of the *shikhara* is modified by the inclusion of wooden beams projecting outwards at an angle to form an 'umbrella' over the shrine. This modification is also evident in the facing Narsingh temple, and probably serves as protection from the weather.

▲ Above: The grand, evocative brass Nandi of Bharmour

▷ Right: Gugga's majestic Ganesh

The benches around Nandi's enclosure are a good place to sit and take in the gentle hum of the complex.

Gugga's other masterpiece here represents **Ganesh**. A local *dhyana*, or hymn, to Ganesh describes this son of Shiva and Parvati thus: 'May the corpulent son of Rudra grant you the desired fruit, he the lord of success and intellect, who alone is quick in destroying and removing obstacles. He, elephant faced and distinguished by an elephant's trunk, bears in his four excellent hands sweetmeats, a rosary, a hatchet and likewise a spotless tusk' (J. Ph. Vogel, *Antiquities of Chamba*, 1994).

Gugga is faithful to tradition, and the god radiates majesty. Unfortunately, like the Nandi outside the Manimahesh whose tail is broken, this sculpture is partially destroyed – its legs are broken.

Finally, the 1.5 m brass **Narsingh** here is a frightening depiction of Vishnu's man-lion incarnation, its jaws open in anger, and its body laden with ornaments. The shrine probably received a grant from Yugakara Varman, Sahila Varman's youngest son. The inscription that records this grant is kept in the Bhuri Singh Museum, and it illuminates the significance attached to religious gifts of land:

'Whatever sin, from birth onward, a man commits, it will be cleansed by a gift of land, be it only the size of cow-hide. He who gives land tilled with the plough, provided with seed corn and fertile, he will be blessed in heaven, as long as light is provided by the sun.

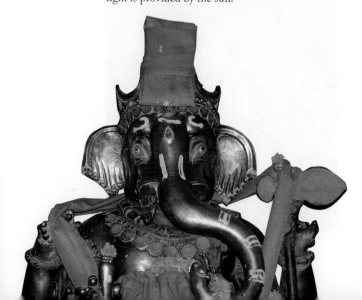

He who takes away [the land] is not cleansed [by digging] a thousand tanks, by hundred horse sacrifices and obligations, and by gift of ten million cows. Those who confiscate a grant of land are born black serpents dwelling in the hollows of withered up trees in waterless forests' (S. L. Nagar).

The grant also records that the temple was built by Queen Tribhuvanrekha *c.* 950-960 AD. Scholars have speculated that the image of Narsingh pre-dates the shrine by at least two centuries, and its creation has been attributed by some scholars to an anonymous artisan from the mid 8th century.

Along the temple's outer façade, there are several representations of small shrines, each with its own deity. The river goddesses Ganga and Yamuna flank the entrance.

The main deity, Narsingh, is the fourth incarnation of Vishnu, half-man and half-lion, who came to rid the earth of Hiranyakashyap, an evil king whom no human could kill. However M.R Thakur, in *Myths, Rituals and Beliefs in Himachal Pradesh*, argues that Narsingh is also one of the *bavan birs*, or 52 heroes, popular among womenfolk throughout the state: 'His temples are thronged by barren women who want an issue or women who

◁ Left: The *shikhara* Narsingh temple

Above: An awe-inspiring sculpture of Vishnu's man-lion incarnation

are desirous of having a son'. An incantation to the deity begins 'O my Narsingha, O great Niranjan, you have captivated me; you have captivated the whole world. Where the maids and virgins are, there is your home...'

Narsingh is sometimes worshipped in the form of a coconut, decorated with a *tilak* of sandalwood paste and honoured with flowers and incense.

The other temples of Chaurasi, most with *lingas* of stone, make this complex a serene haven not only for religion, but also for faith – in nature, myth and, most of all, humanity.

A walk of approximately 4 kms leads to the temple of **Brahmani Devi**, Bharmour's local deity. The location offers stunning views.

There are several legends about the Devi. One tells of how she lived here with her son, who was inordinately fond of his pet bird. When the bird was killed, the boy too died of grief. His mother, in deep mourning, buried herself alive. It is then that villagers found themselves haunted by the spirit of Brahmani Devi, and built a shrine to alleviate her sorrow – so the village acquired its ancient name, Brahmapura: the land of Brahmani.

The Devi's stone image stands exposed to the skies because, it is believed, the goddess caused lightning to strike the temple roof several times, as an indication of her desire to stand free.

Another legend relates that Shiva decreed that all those who undertook the pilgrimage to Manimahesh must break journey to bathe in the sacred pool of Brahmani Devi. The edict is obeyed to this day.

TEMPLES AROUND BHARMOUR: CHHATRARI AND HARSAR

Rivalling the Lakshana Devi brass image in execution, style and state of preservation is Chhatrari's **Shakti Devi**.

Under 50 kms from Chamba, Chhatrari is reached via a detour from Luna village. In a land where surprising, sudden twists in the road that change the scenery are commonplace, the drive to Chhatrari remains startling. The steep 8 kms climb along a narrow, rocky road seems to wind endlessly, until a sharp turn reveals the village in all its perfect, miniature glory. Fields of green colour the formerly stark landscape, as village houses hover cheerfully behind. A walk through slender paths goes through back lanes, behind homes, to the centre where the Shakti Devi complex has stood for over a millennium.

◀ Left: The dazzling Shakti Devi, and a detail from the sculpture

▼ Below: A stone Nandi faces the temple entrance

The temple was originally wooden, though of the earlier construction only the sanctum and a surrounding gallery now remain. Its *pradakshina patha* has 12 grand pillars of wood, elegantly decorated but, unfortunately, corroded. At the entrance, a frieze depicts two crouching lions, and within is the radiant Shakti Devi.

Shakti Devi stands on a lotus, its petals ripe and full. Her slim body, like the Lakshana Devi sculpture, has three folds on the belly – traditional marks of beauty. From the waist down, she is covered with a shimmering skirt, and a belt of pearls circles her waist.

The goddess is covered in modern clothing and jewellery, and much of her original beauty is hidden. Still, she remains impressive: an overwhelming array of jewellery covers her body – a grand crown on her head, earrings and richly formed flowers around the ears, a large, flat necklace. A gentler aspect of the Goddess, she holds a lance, a lotus, a bell and a snake in her four hands.

Possibly Gugga's finest work, the creation of Shakti Devi is associated with a miracle. It is said that after the craftsman built a mansion for the Rana of Bharmour, the landlord had one of his hands cut off, so that no replica of his house

▲ Above: Another view of the beautiful Devi

▼ Below, left and right: The temple's wooden walls and ceiling are covered with carved details

would ever exist. However, when the time came to make the idol at Chhatrari, the Devi herself desired that Gugga mould her form, and so restored his hand. If the legend indicates that Gugga was handicapped when he produced this image, then its beauty is only short of miraculous.

Interestingly, the temple also has a number of other, smaller brass figures which 'remain unnoticed by the few visitors to Chhatrari, overshadowed as they are by the large Shakti icon; besides they are usually dressed in stiff silken garments which conceal their antiquity, and the priests uncover them only after much persuasion' (M. Postel *et al*, *Antiquities of Himachal*, 1985).

▲ Above: A travelling ascetic in the temple compound

▶ Right: Decorations within the shrine include depictions of Vishnu's ten avatars and stories from Krishna's life

These include a bust of Shiva, made in the
'authoritative, imperial style' of 8th century
Kashmir. The torso is V-shaped, the face strong
and square. Shiva's matted hair is covered by a
diadem; and his third eye once had a gem; the
other two are inlaid with electrum (M. Postel).

There is also a small, 20-cms brass statue of
Mahishasurmardini standing on the vanquished
demon, the sculpture worn smooth by centuries
of worship.

◀ Left: The *trimurti* Shiva in the Shakti Devi compound

▼ Below left: Detail from the Shiva temple

▼ Below right: Carved details kept outside the Shakti Devi shrine

▼ Bottom: The ancient Shakti Devi temple

Most interesting are two female figures, rather short and somewhat rounded. Each holds a fruit, and it has been speculated that the shorter one is the Buddhist Tara. This has led some scholars to suggest that Chhatrari may once have had a whole complex of temples, to which these icons belonged; and that at least one of those temples was Buddhist.

Currently, however, there are only two other shrines here: a small, open Shiva *linga*; and a slightly bigger temple to the three-headed, or *trimurti*, Shiva, accompanied by Parvati and Nandi.

Another, somewhat later indication of Buddhist influence in the region occurs about 3 kms down the road from Bharmour to Chamba. A pretty rivulet crosses the road, and nearby there is a rock on which three deities are carved. These are Mahishasurmardini, Shiva before Nandi and Ganesh. Alongside, there are Tibetan inscriptions.

BHARMOUR

41

Approximately 12 kms beyond Bharmour, in the direction of the holy Manimahesh lake and the last stop before the pilgrimage-trek begins, is the village of **Harsar**. A small shrine here holds a brass image of Shiva, a bust with two arms. The sculpture is dated to the 16-17th centuries.

Held just after Janmashtami in August/September, the annual Manimahesh Yatra is so popular that it has been deemed a state level fair in Himachal Pradesh.

△ Above: A bridge across the Budhil

△ Above right: Harsar's Shiva temple

▽ Below: Young boys run with their flock

The pious journey begins from the Lakshmi-Narayana complex in Chamba town and progresses by road to Harsar. From here, pilgrims must follow a mountain track for about 16 kms to the Manimahesh lake, at an altitude of over 4,000 m. The peak measures 5,656 m. The devout are undeterred by the hard terrain however, and the march is usually accompanied by the singing of religious hymns. At the lake, pilgrims bathe in the clear, holy water.

Harsar also has some lovely walks along the Budhil tributary, the landscape clear for miles.

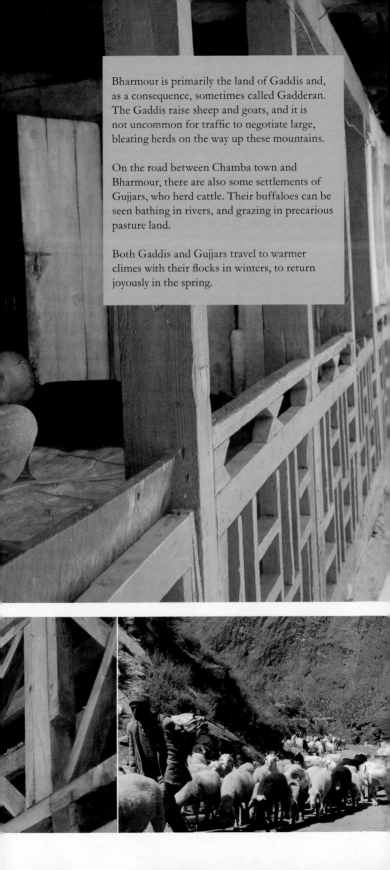

Bharmour is primarily the land of Gaddis and, as a consequence, sometimes called Gadderan. The Gaddis raise sheep and goats, and it is not uncommon for traffic to negotiate large, bleating herds on the way up these mountains.

On the road between Chamba town and Bharmour, there are also some settlements of Gujjars, who herd cattle. Their buffaloes can be seen bathing in rivers, and grazing in precarious pasture land.

Both Gaddis and Gujjars travel to warmer climes with their flocks in winters, to return joyously in the spring.

CHAMBA

Founded by Sahila Varman sometime between 920-940 AD, Chamba is Himachal's hidden gem. Its topography is less easily navigable than that of more popular destinations such as Manali or Dharamshala, but for those willing to make the effort, the district presents delightful spectacles, tiny villages and grand peaks in the background, colourful wildflowers blooming in woods of deodar and pine as birdsong rises gently above the gushing of the deep, royal blue Ravi.

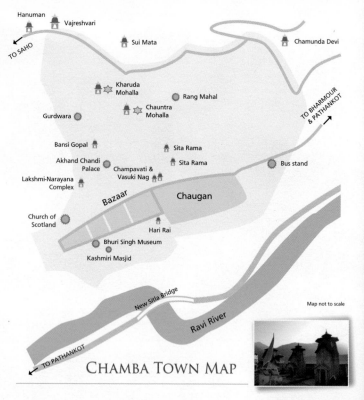

Hanuman
Vajreshvari
TO SAHO
Sui Mata
Chamunda Devi
Kharuda Mohalla
Rang Mahal
Chauntra Mohalla
Gurdwara
TO BHARMOUR & PATHANKOT
Bansi Gopal
Sita Rama
Akhand Chandi Palace
Sita Rama
Champavati & Vasuki Nag
Lakshmi-Narayana Complex
Bus stand
Bazaar
Chaugan
Church of Scotland
Hari Rai
Bhuri Singh Museum
Kashmiri Masjid
New Sitla Bridge
Ravi River
Map not to scale
TO PATHANKOT

CHAMBA TOWN MAP

'Since 1947 [a] motor road, passing along the Ravi gorge deep below it, connects Dalhousie... with Chamba town, and a beautiful bridle path leads to the same place, through a wonderful deodar forest and over the charming mountain lake of Khajjiar, with its romantic snake temple' (Hermann Goetz, *The Early Wooden Temples of Chamba,* 1955).

Approximately 56 kms from Dalhousie at a height of 996 m, Chamba town is accessible by road. The district capital is built on two terraces, and on the lower one is the town 'square', the Chaugan. This large maidan was levelled in 1890 by the British, for use as a promenade and cricket ground. Today it is best known as the site of the annual Minjar Mela (*See p. 62-63*).

▼ Below: A small Nag Temple on the road to Chamba town

Of the two roads that lead to Chamba, the one that runs above the Ravi is certainly more beautiful. Along this route, the river looks like a lagoon – its waters stilled by the Chamera dam. The views are stunning, the river's blue against the white peaks of the Pir Panjal; miraculously perfect brooks that compel silence; villages in the distance, perched with charming insouciance along terraced fields of green and gold; perhaps the passage of a shepherd leading his flock in a setting that gives even the bleating of goats a certain tonality.

A detour of about 14 kms via the dam leads to the **Bhalei Mata** temple, dedicated to Bhadra Kali. At a height of over 1,100 m, the site has breathtaking views. The temple deity, a black stone image, is believed to have been found through a dream revelation in the 16th century. Raja Pratap Singh dreamt that the Devi wanted him to excavate a site approximately 3 kms from Bhalei, where he would find her image. The Raja followed these instructions, and indeed an idol was unearthed. On the return journey, the king and his retinue halted at Bhalei, only to discover that they could no longer pick up the stone image. This was taken as a sign that the Devi wanted to reside here, and accordingly a temple was built at the spot. It was renovated in the 20th century by Raja Sri Singh. In 1973, the image was stolen; but later recovered. It is believed that, since the theft, the idol sometimes perspires.

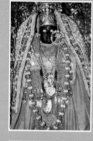

▲ Above: Bhalei Mata

▽ Below: A view of the Ravi from Bhalei Mata temple

From Bhalei Mata, the road heads to Chamba. The Chaugan and the Akhand Chandi Palace are clearly visible, and even the gilded spires of the Lakshmi-Narayana temple may catch one's eye, but in every other respect Chamba resembles a fairly typical small town. It is only with time and exploration that the visitor will realise how the crowded town is suffused with history and art.

Top: The Lakshmi Narayana complex, set against a mountain view

LAKSHMI-NARAYANA

Of its many temples, both in wood and stone, the most well known is Lakshmi-Narayana. It has six main shrines dedicated variously to Shiva, Vishnu and Krishna. The main temple, Lakshmi-Narayana, was built in the 10th century by Sahila Varman, and the white marble image of Vishnu inside was carved from stone brought from the Vindhyas. Nine of the Raja's ten sons perished in the endeavour, and the sculpture bears as much testimony to the god as to Sahila Varman's devotion. The Raja has an almost legendary status in Chamba's royal genealogy, and it is said that the capital he founded had 'an establishment of temples such as no place in the Himalaya between Kashmir and Kumaon could boast of in his time' (Goetz).

Detail from the throne of Lakshmi-Narayana

▼ Below: The grand Vishnu idol in the main Lakshmi-Narayana shrine

All the temples in the Lakshmi-Narayana group are of the *shikhara* style, their graceful sloping roofs and gilded spires glowing in the soft morning light. The entrance to the main shrine is flanked by figures of Ganga and Yamuna, with their respective mounts, a crocodile and tortoise. Inside, the walls are decorated with scenes from the epics. There is also an interesting figure of Vishnu, in which six gods (and not just Brahma, as traditionally held) are shown emerging from six lotus flowers in his navel.

LAKSHMI-NARAYAN TEMPLE COMPLEX: SITE MAP

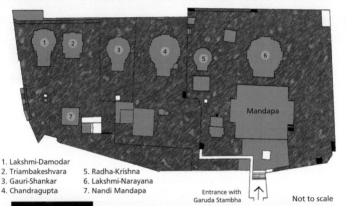

1. Lakshmi-Damodar
2. Triambakeshvara
3. Gauri-Shankar
4. Chandragupta
5. Radha-Krishna
6. Lakshmi-Narayana
7. Nandi Mandapa

Mandapa

Entrance with
Garuda Stambha

Not to scale

◁ Left: Details from the
outer walls of Lakshmi-
Narayana temple

A favourite among Chamba's rulers, the complex
received many grants (many of which are now
stored in the town's Bhuri Singh Museum). An
interesting story concerns Raja Pratap Singh
Varman's (1559-1586) desire to restore the
temples without taxing his subjects. Unable to
find a solution, he was sleeping fitfully when
Narayana himself appeared in a dream and
assured the king that he would find the resources
he needed. And indeed, the very next day a
delegation came to court, bringing news of a
newly discovered copper mine.

The other Vaishnava temples in the complex are dedicated to Lakshmi-Damodar and Radha-Krishna. The latter is crowned with a *chakra*, with white marble figures of Radha and Krishna inside. Lakshmi-Damodar also has a *chakra* crown, and a wooden *mandapa*. Inside, a three-headed Vishnu (in the Vaikuntha style, with human, lion and boar heads) has Lakshmi on his lap, her hand placed gently over his shoulder. There is also a sculpture of Surya, as well as some erotic sculptures.

▲ Above: An elevated Garuda at the entrance to Lakshmi-Narayana

▶ Right: The entrance to the complex

▼ Below: The temple complex in earlier days

The complex has three Shaiva shrines: Chandragupta, Gauri-Shankar and Triambakeshvara. Of these Gauri-Shankar has the most beautifully sculpted bronze deities – Shiva stands with an arm around Parvati, who is decorated with ornaments, a waistband and a garland of flowers. Shiva, naked from the waist up, has a snake wrapped around him.

⌃ Top: A benign, white Nandi graces the complex.

⌃ Above: Detail of the intricate carvings on the outer walls of Lakshmi-Narayan temple

Beautifully sculpted image of Gauri-Shankar in the sanctum of the temple

Chandragupta has the divine couple seated on Nandi, and flanked by Ganesha holding a rod and sweets. Triambakeshvara has a more abstract deity, the *chaturmukha linga* on a *yoni*. Its entrance has Ganga and Yamuna, holding water vessels and heavily ornamented with jewellery and flowers.

The complex is a ten minute walk up a steep road from the main bazaar, and today under the jurisdiction of the Archaeological Survey of India. Photography is prohibited.

53

CHAMUNDA DEVI

One of Chamba's oldest shrines is Chamunda
Devi. Also protected by the ASI, it is sometimes
dated to the 11th century, but may even pre-date
Sahila Varman. The temple is situated along
Chamba's upper terrace. It can be reached on foot
– a half-hour trek from the bus stand – but the
hills are steep and some visitors may prefer to hire
a taxi.

This wooden, pentroof temple is dedicated to the
fierce Chamunda, a name given to Kali because of
her victory over two demons, Chanda and Munda
in the grand battle the Supreme Devi and her
shaktis waged against Shumbha and Nishumbha.

▼ Below left: Detail of
a carved wooden panel
in Chamunda Devi

▼ Below: The ancient
temple itself

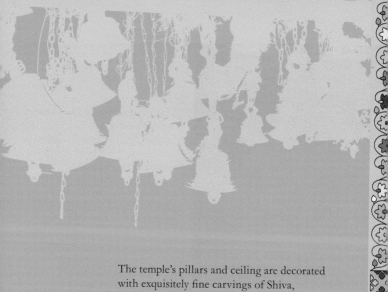

The temple's pillars and ceiling are decorated with exquisitely fine carvings of Shiva, Mahishasurmardini and other gods such as Surya, as well as more lay images.

A grand brass bell at its entrance has tolled the faith of devotees through the centuries, and innumerable smaller bells are strung along its right verandah, behind which the Ravi meanders down its course from Bharmour. On the other side, there is a magnificent view of Chamba, the town – its Chaugan, palace and even temples are clearly visible.

Behind the temple is a small Shiva shrine.

❤ Below: Stone images placed in the Chamunda Devi complex

SUI MATA, VAJRESHVARI AND HANUMAN

A five minute drive from Chamunda Devi is the Sui Mata temple, a modest but touching tribute to Sahila Varman's queen. Queen Sunayana was buried alive, having willingly agreed to sacrifice her life to propitiate the gods and thus bring water to the newly formed capital. The temple, approached by a series of stone steps constructed later, marks the spot where the queen stopped to rest on the way to her death. An uncannily evocative bust of the queen, also known as Sui Mata, is in the sanctum of the shrine. The temple is also the site of the annual Sui Mata fair, celebrated by women in April-May.

A short drive ahead is the 11th century Vajreshvari temple, worth visiting for its striking sculpture and inscriptions – of which there are several on the temple walls. It has a carved stone image of Mahishasurmardini. The temple was probably renovated by Udai Singh in the late 17th century. It is built on a platform, and has wooden *chhatris*.

There is a small Hanuman temple nearby, in the village of Sarotha. The main sculpture of Hanuman is considered very beautiful.

There are also images of Rama and Sita, and his three brothers, Lakshman, Shatrugana and Bharat – as well as skilfully carved representations of other deities.

Recently, this monument, which is maintained by the ASI, was covered with a new tin roof, to protect its sanctum from the rain.

Right: The Hari Rai temple

HARI RAI

Besides the Sui Mata fair, Chamba's most important fair, of course, is the Minjar Mela. One of the stories told about the origin of this week-long extravaganza centres around the Hari Rai temple. It is said that once the Ravi flowed along this temple, located to the northwestern corner of the Chaugan. One sage alone would brave the waters daily for his meditation, until Sahila Varman asked him to make the temple more accessible. The holy man went into a deep trance that lasted a week, during which time he also wove a cord – the original *minjar*. On awakening, he threw the cord into the river, upon which the Ravi changed its course.

Hari Rai is now eminently accessible, and its Vishnu in Vaikuntha form is sometimes held to be the region's most beautiful sculpture. Clad in a *dhoti*, decorated with wonderful jewellery and with silver eyes, the image may be older than the shrine it inhabits, dating to the 9-10th centuries, while the temple belongs to the 11th century.

The shrine is relatively small, a *shikhara* temple made of stone. Its walls are carved with numerous motifs, including deities such as Surya, Shiva and his consort, and images of amorous couples.

⌃ Top left: Sui Mata Devi

⌃ Above left: A view of the Sui Mata shrine from below

◁ Left: Water flows at the shrine of a queen who died to save her people from drought

OTHER TEMPLES

There are almost 30 temples in Chamba town, but it is entirely possible for a distracted visitor to pass a thousand year old shrine without noticing it. This very unobtrusiveness, perhaps, gives the town its charm – imbued as it is with faith, it feels no need to put piety on display. It would be a pity, however, if shrines such as the following were left out of travellers' itineraries.

Champavati, an 11th century *shikhara* temple in stone, was built by Sahila Varman for his daughter of the same name. The story goes that Champavati developed great

Detail from the walls of Champavati

faith in a sage who lived at this spot. Her father grew suspicious of her frequent visits to the sage's home. One day, unable to contain himself any longer, he charged into the holy man's abode, his sword drawn, ready to avenge honour.

The house was empty and still. As the Raja stood bemused, a disembodied voice broke the silence. Champavati and the sage had transcended into another realm, it said, to punish the king for his lack of trust. Now, to prevent further misfortune, he was to build a temple to Champavati where he stood.

Another, simpler, story suggests that the temple is named for the many *champak* flowers that grow here. Its presiding deity is Mahishasurmardini.

Close by, though almost forgotten by locals, is the **Vasuki Nag** temple, one of the many Nag shrines in Himachal Pradesh, where the cult of the snake gods has captured popular imagination almost as successfully as Vaishnavism and Shaivism.

There are two **Sita-Rama** temples within ten minutes' walking distance of Vasuki Nag.

Further ahead, above Lakshmi-Narayana is **Bansi Gopal** temple, dedicated to Krishna, who is shown within, playing the flute to his companion Radha. The sculpture on its outer walls reminds some scholars of Khajuraho; and the temple is also decorated with carvings of other deities. Its construction is ascribed to the late 16th century ruler, Balabhadra Varman.

❮ Left: A tiger faces the Champavati shrine

⬘ Above: The Bansi Gopal temple

⬘ Above right: The idol of Krishna playing the flute in the temple's sanctum

⬙ Below: One of many remarkable carvings on the outer walls of Bansi Gopal

Somewhat further up, in Chamba's **Kharuda and Chauntra** *mohallas are* several temples built under Raja Umed Singh in the mid 18th century. These stone *shikhara* shrines may have functioned as memorials to the district's rulers. Their walls have intricate carvings, some of the rajas themselves. Unfortunately, the temples are ill-preserved; some suffered considerable damage during the earthquake of 1905 and the effects of natural corrosion are taking their toll.

OTHER RELIGIOUS MONUMENTS

Though known primarily for its temples, Chamba also has a church, a mosque and a gurdwara. The Church of Scotland is well worth a visit. Founded by Rev. William Ferqueen over a century ago, the church has some impressive stone work, and beautiful lancer arch windows.

The Kashmiri Masjid, painted pale green, stands behind the Bhuri Singh Museum, surrounded by narrow lanes. The Gurdwara is close to the Chauntra *mohalla*.

AKHAND CHANDI PALACE AND RANG MAHAL

Chamba has two royal houses, the Akhand Chandi Palace and the Rang Mahal. Both were built by Umed Singh, who ruled between 1748-1764, though later additions were made to both buildings by rajas and British administrators. For example, Raja Bhuri Singh added a Zenana Mahal to the Akhand Chandi Palace, and Captain Marshall built its Darbar Hall (sometimes also referred to as the Marshall Hall).

◀ Left: A Shiva *linga* in a small shrine within the Bansi Gopal complex

▼ Below: The Rang Mahal

In 1958, the royal family sold the Palace to the Himachal Pradesh Government. Today it is a popular tourist destination for its painted walls, and glass and wood work; as well as the views it affords of Chamba town.

The Rang Mahal, once part royal residence, part granary, is used by the Handicrafts Department of the Government as a workshop for various crafts including *chappal* and *rumaal* making. Most of the paintings have been taken from here and stored in Delhi's National Museum and Chamba's Bhuri Singh Museum, though it is a worthwhile visit for those interested in watching master craftspersons engaged in their work. It also has a small emporium.

CHAMBA

BHURI SINGH MUSEUM

Named after Raja Bhuri Singh (r. 1904-1919), the Museum opened in September 1908. Located about five minutes from the Hari Rai temple, the Museum is open from 10.00 am – 5.00 pm except on Mondays and gazetted holidays. (*For a detailed overview of the Museum see p. 98-101*)

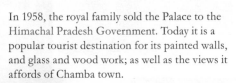

MINJAR MELA

With the status of a state festival, the Minjar Mela attracts numerous tourists and celebrants. The fair lasts a week in July/August, and begins when a flag is hoisted in the Chaugan. People, dressed in their best, and most wearing a *minjar*, or thread of tasselled silk, crowd the central *maidan*, shopping and participating in or watching a variety of competitive and cultural programmes. The Minjar procession marches on the third day and includes local gods, accompanied by dancers, percussionists and the Police and Home Guards.

Originally, the fair was intended to bring a good harvest, and a buffalo would be thrust into the river as a sacrifice. Even if it survived the water and swam to the other bank, this would be construed to mean that the town's sins had been carried across to the other side. Over the years, the buffalo was substituted with a coconut, one Rupee, a fruit and a *minjar*.

◁ Clockwise from top left: Deities such as this goddess travel to the Mela in palanquins; The joyous Minjar Mela procession; Crowds gather in the Chaugan; Stalls set up during the fair; Wrestling matches form part of the celebration

A poster announces Chamba's celebration of its Millennium in 2006

EXCURSIONS

Just on the outskirts of town, the Department of Tourism is creating an **Art Garden** by the Ravi river. Its three grassy lawns are ideal picnic spots. Somewhat further, about 10 kms from Chamba on the Chamba-Tissa road is the enchanting village of **Rajpura**. It has the Mazar of a Sufi saint, Sai Jamal Shah, revered by Hindus and Muslims alike.

About 2 kms from Chamba town is the village of **Obri**, with the 300 year old Banlingeshwar temple, dedicated to Shiva. Built in the pentroof style, the temple's *garbhagriha* has a Shiva *linga* and images of Ganesh, Parvati and Nandi, all carved from stone. It is also notable for the beautiful paintings along its walls.

Somewhat further, 18 kms along the Chamba-Chuari road is **Chuari Jot**, or Pass, at over 2,400 m. In summer, the forests of deodar and kail here are decorated with rhododendrons. This is also the route used for centuries by Gaddis and Gujjars migrating to and from the plains.

▲ Above: Boys play cricket on the outskirts of Chamba town

▼ Below: The Naryana temple, Udaipur

▶ Right: Young boys from Udaipur village

Another interesting excursion from town is **Udaipur**. Less than 10 kms from Chamba, this pretty village might have had nothing more than its gently sloping lanes and brilliant green fields to recommend it, were it not for two facts. The first is its connection with Raja Udai Singh, who ruled Chamba *c.* 1690. It is here that the king and his brother Lakshman Singh were assassinated by a delegation of court officials.

The site of the assassination remains uncultivated to this day – even though its significance is now partially forgotten, and the bare land is used as a playground by students at the village school. A five minute walk away is the Narayana temple, built in honour of the two brothers. This small shrine has a Devi flanked by the king and Lakshman Singh. The carvings on its walls are remarkably well preserved; but its greatest attraction is the setting – a pastoral, almost cinematic paradise.

And in fact, Udaipur's other significance is its connection to Bollywood. A blockbuster of the 1990s, *Taal,* was filmed here, in the building next to the school, which served as a music school for the film's protagonist, Aishwarya Rai.

Perhaps the most beautiful drive out of Chamba town is to the village of **Saho**, about 15 kms away, with two shrines dedicated to Chandrashekhar (Shiva) and Vishnu.

The winding road follows a sparkling, shallow stream of water, which occasionally bursts into miniature waterfalls, its banks lined with orchards of walnut trees. On the other side, it passes through tiny villages, houses and gardens spilling onto the road, rose bushes laden with flowers. Saho itself is fairly spread out, and a narrow path leads through wheat fields to its temple compound.

Chadrashekhar, the larger of the two shrines, looks modern – its slate roof and whitewashed pillars an anomaly in this land of ancient temples. It may have been rebuilt after the floods of 1900. However, the 1.5 m *linga* within, dates to the 10th century; and the story of its origin is equally ancient.

It is believed that a village sage would bathe at the conjunction of two streams nearby. He was

 Top left: A typical roadside scene on the outskirts of Chamba town

 Top right: The fields of Saho

 Above left: The joyous Nandi at Chandrashekhar

 Above centre: The Chandrashekhar temple

 Above right: The rivers that water the district

always the first to bathe, until one day he began to suspect that another was bathing before him. So, the sage hid himself by the stream and, sure enough, as dawn broke, three young boys ran into the stream. The *sadhu* ran after them, and managed to grab hold of one. When questioned, he revealed that his name was Chandrashekhar, and his friends were Mahesh and Chandragupta. Before the *sadhu* could make any further investigations, the boy turned into a *linga*.

It is said that the other two boys ran to Bharmour and Chamba respectively, where they too turned into *lingas* and reside in eponymous shrines.

Chadrashekhar temple's entrance shows Shiva in two forms. The angry Shiva, with three heads, stands on a corpse and wears a garland of skulls. His benign avatar holds a flower, rosary, trident and pot of water in his four arms.

The temple courtyard has a black, stone Nandi facing the shrine. The bull wears a loving, friendly expression, tinged with mischief. A myth tells how long years ago Saho's residents found that an animal was grazing in their fields at night. Hoping to catch the miscreant, an old woman kept guard, and caught the bull in the act of leaving its position. So trapped, Nandi froze, one foot ahead of the other, and has remained in that position since.

A smaller shrine here is dedicated to Vishnu. It shows the god in Vaikuntha form. Lakshmi rises from beneath his feet, while Brahma and Shiva flank his sides. Vishnu's halo is pasted with sand from the Ganges. Smaller images in the temple show Vishnu's ten incarnations.

◁ Left: A beautifully engraved Nandi in the Chandrashekhar sanctum

▽ Below left: Children gather at the temple entrance

▽ Below: A view of the sacred Manimahesh peak, on the road from Chamba town to Dalhousie.

DALHOUSIE:
A POETIC RETREAT

'One of the finest hill station in India is Dalhousie from the beauty point of view, climate and agreeable surroundings.'

(Jawaharlal Nehru)

Nehru was not alone in his love for this quiet hill-station. Rabindranath Tagore came here to write poetry, Subhash Chandra Bose to recover from imprisonment and Bhagat Singh's uncle Ajit Singh, a freedom fighter in his own right, lived and died in Dalhousie.

After the Anglo-Sikh War of 1845, Punjab's rulers were obliged to cede their lands in the hills to the British, as part of war indemnity. Much of the area that now forms Chamba came directly under British control, with Chamba's king paying an annual tribute of Rs. 12,000. For the British, however, weakened by the heat and dust of the plains, Chamba's gentle climate was of greater value. So, over the 1850s, they acquired five hills on the western tip of the Dhauladhar range to create a 'Sanatorium for Europeans'. In return, the raja's tribute was lowered.

Colonel Napier selected the land – the Kathalagh, Potreyn, Terah (or Moti Tibba), Bakrota and Bhangora hills – and Sir Donald McLeod suggested the Sanatorium be named after the Governor General, Lord Dalhousie. Soon enough, the prettily located hill-station became a favourite with those seeking rest and recuperation. The Chamba raja, too, built a palace here in 1870-71, called Jandrighat. The local post office offered a daily service to Chamba town and back. Today, Dalhousie's GPO is a miniature version of Shimla's Mall, with restaurants, a Tibetan bazaar and hotels.

◀ Left: Lord Dalhousie

▼ Below: A café in Gandhi Chowk

Also known as **Gandhi Chowk**, the GPO is the point of departure for many of the town's picturesque tourist sites.

Dalhousie's oldest church, **St. John's**, is here. Built in 1863 under Rev. John H. Pratt, this Protestant church still holds a service every Sunday. Unfortunately, that is the only day of the week it is open, so many visitors must content themselves with its exterior. Nevertheless, this modest, gently rounded building set in a lovingly manicured lawn exerts a quiet influence over the busy Chowk, emitting a note of tranquillity on which the chatter of tourists and gossip of locals rests easily.

Just adjacent to St. John's is the **Raizada Hansraj Sondhi Memorial Library**, named after the man credited with reviving Dalhousie post-Independence. Hansraj Sondhi, a loyal resident of the hill-station realised, to his chagrin, that Dalhousie was becoming increasingly neglected. Barely a few years after Independence, in the early 1950s, 400 of the 485 houses in Dalhousie were uninhabited.

Fortunately, Hansraj Sondhi was a friend of Jawaharlal Nehru, and he appealed to the Prime Minister to visit the town. Nehru complied, and was pained by the obvious neglect from which this pretty hill-station was suffering.

So, measures to repopulate and repopularise Dalhousie were suggested, and implemented – in effect bringing the town back to life, much as its gentle breezes and magnificent views had once helped convalescents regain strength.

▲ Above: The Dhauladhar range by Alfred Hallett, *c.* 1980

▼ Below: A view of the Pir Panjal

▲ Above: A tree of peace in Panchpula

▼ Below: The serene St. John's Church

Perhaps the most famous of them was Subhash Chandra Bose. The nationalist leader came here to recover from pleurisy, contracted during a long period of imprisonment. Between May and October 1937, he lived with Dr. Dharamveer, a family friend, at Kynance, a beautiful home some distance from the GPO. His daily walks would take him to a fresh water pond, hidden amid cedar woods, where he would often pause for a drink of water. Today this pond, a gentle 1 km walk from the GPO, has been christened **Subhash Baoli**. Both the walk, with its uninterrupted views of snow-capped peaks, and the quiet pond and its surroundings, remain wonderfully relaxing.

Another freedom fighter is commemorated in **Panchpula**, about 3 kms from the GPO, with a memorial to Sardar Ajit Singh, the charismatic Bhagat Singh's paternal uncle. Ajit Singh is credited with having coined the phrase *Pagri Sambhal Jattha!* (protect your turban, young man!), which became an anti-imperialist war-cry across Punjab in the early 20th century.

Dalhousie is known for its churches. Besides St. John's, these include St. Andrew's, St. Francis' and St. Patrick's. **St. Andrew's**, also known as the Church of Scotland, is charmingly unassuming, and located slightly out of town in the cantonment area. Also in the cantonment, near the military hospital, is **St. Patrick's**, Dalhousie's largest church with a seating capacity of 300.

▲ Above: Inside St. Francis' Church

◀ Left: Subhash Chowk

▼ Below: Stained glass window from St. Francis´ Church

▼ Bottom: An example of the stunning views for which Dalhousie is famed

St. Francis' Church is more accessible, located on a hill on Dalhousie's second main square, **Subhash Chowk**, this Catholic church holds a Mass every Sunday morning. Inside, it has some lovely painted glass windows, as well as beautiful stone and wood work. The priest's residence is behind the church; and a few steps further is the Sacred Heart School, established in 1910 by Belgian nuns and still a popular boarding school.

The **Radha Soami Satsang Bhawan and Hospital** is approximately 300 m from Gandhi Chowk. Also nearby is **Shivkul**, a spiritual ashram which also affords splendid views of the Pir Panjal range.

Such views, and the walks that afford them, are integral to Dalhousie. The hills are gentle and trekking here is a lazy, meditative activity. Within town, for example, the Gandhi and Subhash Chowks are connected by two mall roads – Thandi Sadak and Garam Sadak (cold and warm roads).

Thandi Sadak, so named because it receives minimal sunshine, is broad and green; lined on one side by old buildings and hotels and on the other by high mountains, snow glistening on their peaks. From certain points on this road it is even possible to glimpse the Pangi range, Chamba's most isolated district. **Garam Sadak**, in contrast, is narrow and sunny, slightly more wild, with flowers and rhododendron trees blooming in myriad colours.

Some rocks along Garam Sadak are beautifully painted by Dalhousie's fairly significant Tibetan community. Images of Padmasambhava and Avalokiteshvara add colour to the road. From Subhash Chowk, a motorable road leads to the bus stand, via a Tibetan bazaar. Another tiny lane winds down to **Sadar Bazaar**, known for its gold and silver jewellery; and a small temple. There is also a yoga institute here, called **Dakshina Murti**.

A somewhat longer and steeper walk goes up to **Bakrota hill**, Dalhousie's highest peak, from where, on clear days, the deep blue Ravi river is visible. About half way up, 5 kms from Gandhi Chowk, is **Norwood Paramdham**, a house prettily located in a forest of deodars.

▲ Top: Buddhist murals line Garam Sadak

▼ Below: Another fabulous view from Dalhousie

Twice a year, devotees of Swami Satyananda, who meditated here in 1925, converge to the site for grand *satsangs*. At the turn to Norwood, a plaque commemorates Rabindranath Tagore's visit.

Visitors may also choose to walk down to the cantonment, for its two churches and a serene, old graveyard, dating to British times.

On clear nights, Dalhousie becomes almost magical. A deep quiet descends, and stars illuminate the town. It is even said that, occasionally, the view extends to the lights twinkling in Lahore.

EXCURSIONS

About 12 kms before Dalhousie is **Banikhet**, which has a 150-year-old Nag temple, and the residential colony of the Chamba Hydroelectric Project.

In the opposite direction, about 10 kms from Gandhi Chowk up Bakrota hill is **Lakkar Mandi**, traditionally inhabited by Dogra families who once made a living making charcoal. Changing circumstances, however, have enforced a change in their livelihood, and now most work as migrant labour, and the village is uninhabited for much of the year. From Lakkar Mandi, two roads diverge. One leads up about 3 kms through **Kalatop**. This wildlife sanctuary, located in dense forests of pine and deodar, is a wonderful retreat. Though it is possible to drive through it (a car permit costs Rs. 100), the better option is to walk.

A forest guide accompanies visitors, and it is possible to spot a variety of wildlife here, including black bears. The chirping of birds and the scent of wild flowers follows walkers along the trail, which goes via a small Shiva *linga*, strategically placed at a point from which there is a view of the Manimahesh peak. At its peak, Kalatop has a forest rest house on a small meadow, which can be booked through the DFO (Wildlife) Chamba, at Rs. 500 per night.

The second road from Lakkar Mandi leads to **Khajjiar**, a little over 20 kms from Dalhousie and about half-way to Chamba. This large

⌃ Above: An idol of Hanuman at the Baniket temple

⌃ Top Right: The Forest Guest House in Kalatop

⌄ Below: The Khajjiar meadow and lake

meadow, surrounded by pine forests and with a natural pond at its centre is a popular picnic spot, complete with fast food and pony rides. There is also an ancient Nag temple here, built about the 12th century. Within are five intriguing wooden statues of the Pandava brothers, commissioned by Raja Balabhadra Varman in the 16th century. On two adjacent sides of the Nag temple are small shrines to Shiva and Hadimba Devi (the demoness consort of Bhima).

Several hotels around the meadow provide accommodation to those wishing to make Khajjiar more than a day's outing.

Another hour's drive through picture perfect scenery leads to Chamba – the district capital and a treasure trove of ancient temples, stunning landscapes and more.

PANGI: A SECLUDED PARADISE

The Pangi sub-division forms a kind of crown over Chamba district. This valley, formed by the Chandrabhaga, which descends from the confluence of the Chandra and Bhaga rivers in Upper Lahaul, is cut off from Chamba by soaring white peaks for most of the year and can only be visited in the short summer months.

▲ Clockwise from above: The sun shines through clouds in Pang Woodwork on the wal of Mindhal Mata; The Mindhal Mata temple

And yet, for those who do brave the terrain and visit the valley, 'Pangi is unique in its grandeur and beauty.... on the lower ranges are grassy slopes or rich pasture with dense forests of pine and cedar, while high over all, the stern and majestic mountains, piled on one another... [rise] far beyond the line of eternal snow' (*Gazetteer of the Chamba State, 1904*).

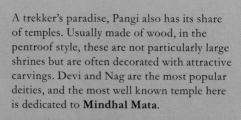

A trekker's paradise, Pangi also has its share of temples. Usually made of wood, in the pentroof style, these are not particularly large shrines but are often decorated with attractive carvings. Devi and Nag are the most popular deities, and the most well known temple here is dedicated to **Mindhal Mata**.

Located slightly over 12 kms from Killar, the headquarters of the sub-divsion, the Mindhal Mata temple stands on the banks of the Chandrabhaga. Its sanctum has a small brass idol of Mindhal Mata, who is said to have revealed herself to an old woman of the village. The Devi came to her in the form of a black stone in the fireplace. But, when the woman's sons and neighbours refused to believe her, the Devi, in her anger, turned them all to stone. Later, the Devi decreed that the old woman would be worshipped by those who came to pray at the Mindhal Mata shrine.

Made of alternating wood and stone, this pentroof temple has some beautiful carvings on its outer walls. It is also decorated with numerous bells.

Three other temples of note are located together in Sach village, a fair distance south of Killar. The shrines are dedicated to Nageshwar, Phroad Nag and Shiva.

Built by Sach's residents themselves, the **Nageshwar** temple enshrines a metal image of Nag Devta, as well as many carvings on its wooden walls. At the temple's entrance, several animal horns hung on the walls indicate the practice of ritual animal sacrifice here. In the nearby temple of **Phroad Nag**, the sanctum contains numerous tridents. The main idol of Nag Devta is made of stone.

In Killar itself, there is the Detnag temple. Also known as **Dehantnag**, the shrine is dedicated to a black image of Nag, said to have travelled here all the way from Lahaul. Its location, amidst a grove of cedar trees, is peaceful – and in fact, many of Pangi's shrines are built within a group of such trees.

Somewhat further, towards Jammu and Kashmir and near Luj village is the temple of **Sitla Mata**. The wooden temple's *garbhagriha* has a brass image of the Devi. Outside, a trident has been carved on its roof. A small *maidan* near the temple is used for the annual Sitla Mata fair.

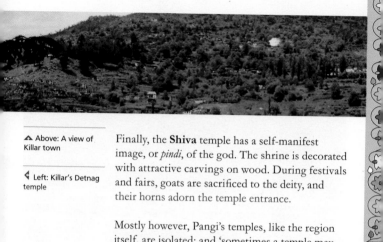

▲ Above: A view of Killar town

◀ Left: Killar's Detnag temple

Finally, the **Shiva** temple has a self-manifest image, or *pindi*, of the god. The shrine is decorated with attractive carvings on wood. During festivals and fairs, goats are sacrificed to the deity, and their horns adorn the temple entrance.

Mostly however, Pangi's temples, like the region itself, are isolated; and 'sometimes a temple may be found within the interior of a forest or in some mountain ravine, standing quite alone' (V. Verma, *Pangi: A Tribal Habitat in Mid-Himalaya*). So, visitors are likely to find *padukas*, or footprint pillars, placed on the road to a temple. These pillars consist of a pile of stones covered with a flat slab, on which is carved the image of a trident, with footprints on either side. Not only do *padukas* indicate the way to a shrine, they also allow devotees to offer their prayers without the long, often arduous journey to the temple itself.

◀ Left: The Nag temple at Sach

◀ Left below: A small shrine along the Sach pass

▼ Below: Another view of Killar, surrounded by pine trees and high mountains

And so, all visitors to Pangi must discover the region for themselves, the warm heart of this austere, secluded land, where 'myth is history and mystery is reality' – and where lofty mountains and powerful gods watch over the people (Minakshi Chaudhari, *Exploring Pangi Himalaya: A World Beyond Civilisation*).

PAINTING IN CHAMBA

Chamba, an ancient princely state situated in the difficult mountainous terrains of the north-western Himalayas, had the rare fortune of preserving its rich cultural heritage from Islamic invaders. The rulers of Chamba were connoisseurs of the arts and they encouraged artists and craftsmen, extending them generous and sustained patronage, which resulted in fine specimens of art and architecture.

▶ Rignt: Fig. 1, Raja Balabhadra Varman

The art of painting originated in Chamba in the first half of the 17th century. A surviving portrait of Raja Balabhadra Varman (r. 1589-1641) now in the collection of the State Museum, Shimla (fig. 1) indicates an early tradition of the art of painting in Chamba. Other direct evidence pertaining to painting activity in Chamba during the mid 17th century includes the figures engraved on the copper pedestal of Hadimba Devi temple at Mehla, (fig. 2) which was commissioned by Raja Prithvi Singh (r. 1641-1664). This prince is said to have embellished the 'State-Kothi' of Bharmour with splendid wood carvings depicting figural work inspired by Mughal art. A wooden door acquired from the State-Kothi and now preserved in the Bhuri Singh Museum shows young Prithvi Singh standing in front of prince Dara Shikoh portrayed as falconer on the other panel of the door (fig. 3).

We know of some Gujarati-Manikanth painters working at the Chamba court during the reign of Raja Chhatra Singh (1664-90), and the visage of this Raja has come down to us in several portraits. The portraits of this Raja and his contemporaries, Miyan Jai Singh and Shakat Singh, as well as some other paintings illustrating various themes – *Dasavatara*, *Ragamala* and *Nayika-Bheda* – evidence a mature painting style having distinct characteristics practised at Chamba. Since the *Dasavatara* theme was popular in Chamba, it was repeatedly depicted in stray miniatures and wall paintings, metal sheets and wood carvings. An early and dispersed *Dasavatara* series from a Chamba workshop, dateable to the late 17th century, is of special relevance. A folio from this work depicting Kalki is reproduced here as figure 4.

⌃ Top: Fig. 2, detail of copper engraving

⌃ Above: Fig. 3, Dara Shikoh, the Mughal prince

‹ Left: Fig. 4, the Kalki avatar

Chamba paintings of the early 18th century depict a mature and indigenous painting style with distinct characteristics. One sees male figures wearing a typical crown with triangular motifs and a *dhoti* with a particular kind of shading using parallel lines. Male figures also bear long horizontal *tilaka* marks on their foreheads, have elongated almond-shaped eyes with reddish corners, and circular forms that indicate prominent chest muscles. These traits continued in practice in the Chamba painting style, though in a slightly refined manner, until the mid 18th century.

In the first quarter of the 18th century we find the Chamba style imbibing the idioms and traits of the neighbouring states of Nurpur and Basohli. A folio from a dispersed Chamba Ragamala series depicting 'Ragaputra Sarang' from the Bhuri Singh Museum collection confirms this suggestion. Local Chamba painters continued painting in this style until the reign of Raja Umed Singh (r. 1748-64).

Raja Umed Singh was an ardent devotee of the goddess Chamunda and he constructed the temple dedicated to the great goddess at the Devi-ki-Kothi village in Chamba's Churah region in 1754. He embellished this temple with exquisite wood carvings and murals done in the local Chamba style, which are credited to the carpenter-artisans Gurdev and Jhanda. Several portraits of this prince are extant (fig. 5).

⌃ Above: Fig. 5, Raja Umed Singh

⌃ Top: Fig 6, the Matsya avatar

⌃ Top right: Fig 7, Krishna in combat with the serpent Kaliya

▶ Right: Fig 8, A folio from the *Ramayana* shows king Dashratha with the god Agni

Another talented painter from Chamba was Mahesh. A *Dasavatara* set painted by him is known and one of the folios of this dispersed set depicting Matsya avatar explicitly shows his artistic skill (fig. 6). Mahesh was a gifted portrait painter as revealed by some portrait studies done by him.

Another important series of the *Bhagvata Purana* was painted by Laharu in 1758 at the instance of Miyan Shamsher Singh (Raja Umed Singh's younger brother) as revealed by a Takri inscription on the last picture of this set. An example from this extensive *Bhagavata* series, exhibiting the style of Laharu, is shown as figure 7.

Laharu and Mahesh were gifted painters who, perhaps, worked jointly in the workshop of the Gujarati painters. Raja Umed Singh also commissioned a series on the *Ramayana*, but only a part, *Balakanda* (fig. 8) and *Ayodhyakanda*, was completed during his lifetime. Architectural edifices dominate these *Ramayana* paintings. Conical trees with thick foliage are arrayed in rows upon rocky grounds. Male figures, particularly courtiers and retainers, are shown wearing richly patterned and striped *jama* in these pictures.

Raja Umed Singh died at the age of 39 and was succeeded in 1764 by his son Raj Singh, who was nine years old at the time. Evidence reveals that Guler painters received patronage at the Chamba court when Raja Raj Singh was only about 15 years of age. Like his father, he was also a great devotee of Chamunda, the goddess of war. He also commissioned a *Devi Mahatmya* series, which was painted by the Guler painters and is now preserved in the Bhuri Singh Museum. Several portrait studies of Raja Raj Singh are extant.

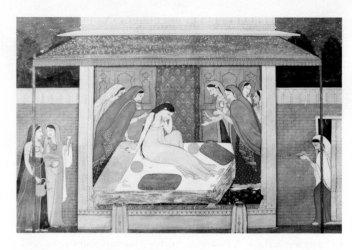

Nikka, the eldest son of the famous Guler painter Nainsukh, was a very talented painter, and was given a land grant in the fertile area of Rilhu within Chamba territory on the Chamba-Kangra border. The family from Guler painted a great deal for the Chamba court and the series of *Rukmini-Mangal*, *Sudama Charit* and *Usha Charit* (fig. 9) are the works rendered by these gifted painter brothers – Nikka and Ranjha.

After the arrival of Guler painters at Chamba, a change can be discerned in the style of local painters. The new trends of Guler painting not only influenced the Chamba style but swept across almost all the centres in the hills. Local Chamba painters started working in the 'new' style, imbibing the pictorial conventions of the Guler style. Two such examples, one depicting a scene of 'Danalila' and another from the *Aranyakanda* (fig. 10) reveal this fact.

⌃ Above right: Jaideva paying homage to Krishna and Radha in a painting by Vijay Sharma

⌃ Above: Fig. 9, 'Usha's dream' from the *Usha Charit*

⌄ Below: Fig. 10, the brothers Rama and Lakshman pursue demons in the *Aranyakanda*

⌄ Below right: Fig. 11, Raja Jit Singh with his queen

In 1793, Raja Raj Singh was succeeded by his son Jit Singh, who was 18 years old at that time. During Jit Singh's reign, no extended series of paintings seem to have been painted in Chamba, except for those related to the subjects of *Ashtanayika* and *Baramasa*. Chhajju and Harkhu were leading Guler painters of this time, settled in Rajol village in the Rilhu area. Chhajju, an artist of considerable merit, painted the likeness of Raja Jit Singh with remarkable perfection (fig. 11). His brother Harkhu was also a gifted painter as apparent in the several competent works done by him. The brush work of these painters is precise and perfect, and the colour scheme employed by them is soft and muted. Besides, the standard Kangra-type treatment in female faces can be noticed in the paintings done by them.

The tradition of miniature painting continued even in the 19th century and it is evident that Guler painters, the grandsons of Nikka, were still rendering their services to the Chamba court. A dated example painted by Attra in 1860 depicting the scene of 'Yama's Court' represents the late Kangra style.

Later, Sohnu and Jawahar were two painters from the Gujarati-Manikanth family active in Chamba in the early 20th century. Some of their works, though lacking refinement, are preserved in the Bhuri Singh Museum.

Prem Lal (d. 1974) was a versatile artist of exceptional merit and he revived the tradition of painting in Chamba. His three sons also paint in Pahari style and are continuing the family tradition. Vijay Sharma is another accomplished artist working at the Bhuri Singh Museum. He paints in most Pahari styles, besides making his own compositions. Presently he is engaged in reviving the tradition of Pahari painting by imparting training to some promising pupils.

ARTS AND CRAFTS

Tucked away in relative isolation, the customs, traditions, arts and crafts of this part of north India have been well preserved, leaving Chamba with an artistic legacy as splendid as its exceptional natural beauty. The Mughals could not extend their territory to this hilly kingdom and their influence remained limited to Chamba's miniature paintings.

Of all the crafts in Chamba, the most famous is that of the **Chamba Rumaal**, a form of embroidery that has been practised in other areas of Himachal Pradesh as well, like Kangra and Basohli. Its present association exclusively with Chamba derives from local rulers who patronised the craft and helped it develop into the intricate beauty it is today. Its *do-rukha* (double) satin stitches with untwisted silken yarn ensure that no knots

▲ Above, below and right: Examples of the wide variety of *rumaals* produced through the ages in Chamba

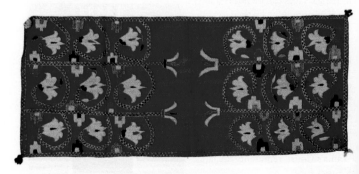

are visible, and the *rumaal* looks exactly the same on both sides. The patterns are a combination of floral and geometrical designs and favourite themes include *Chaupad*, *Raas Leela*, *Shikaar*, and the *Mahabharata*. Human and animal figures are shown in painstaking detail.

Chamba *rumaals* were traditionally used on auspicious occasions to cover ritual offerings, and were given as part of a bride's dowry. Their fine craftsmanship came from two distinct streams: elite ladies of noble households, and womenfolk from rural homes. The *rumaals* were first visualised and outlined, then the colour scheme was decided and finally the cloth was embroidered, a process that remains similar to this day.

Rural women usually decided the outlines and colour schemes themselves, and their creations were bright and contrasting, with less sense of perspective and human anatomy. More elite women had access to talented miniature painters, who drew outlines for them and suggested colour schemes. This is evident in the amazing intricacy of design and subtlety of colours of their *rumaals*.

Chamba was also an important centre of **Pahari Painting**, absorbing painters and their naturalistic Mughal style from the nearby town of Nurpur. Some of these painters were from the Mughal atelier, who chose to migrate to the hills, where they were patronised by local rulers and soon developed original styles of their own.

The Pahari style developed distinct characteristics by the 18th century. With plain backgrounds, little attempt at perspective, stylised human figures, and trees with triangular foliage, these paintings differ from the original Mughal style, but retain some of its elements in, for example depictions of architecture. The figures and faces gradually took on a heavier aspect, the colour tonalities became more bright and exuberant, and today Chamba's miniatures have a singular finesse all their own.

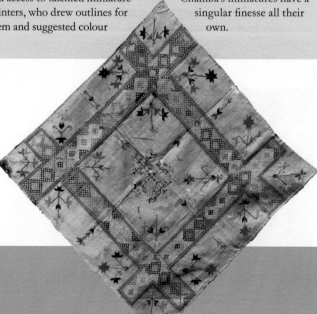

Another fascinating craft of the region is **Metal Craft**, bronze-casting in particular, which was introduced to Chamba by Kashmiri artisans, whose influence is still visible in the local sculptures. Common figures are those of Devi, Ganesh, Gauri Shankar and Narsingh, and some of the best examples are found in Bharmour and Chamba town. The method used for casting is age-old, the Cire Perdu, whereby a wax image is first created then coated thinly with clay leaving a hole to pour in liquid metal. The clay is hardened through baking in a fire, which lets the wax melt away, leaving an empty shell of clay. Liquid bronze is poured into this shell, and allowed to cool, thus taking the shape of the image. Finally, the clay is removed to reveal the image, which is sculpted and polished further to refine its features. Its eyes are often inlaid with silver.

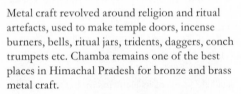

▲ Above: The magnificent Shakti Devi, one of the best examples of Chamba's metal crafting tradition

Metal craft revolved around religion and ritual artefacts, used to make temple doors, incense burners, bells, ritual jars, tridents, daggers, conch trumpets etc. Chamba remains one of the best places in Himachal Pradesh for bronze and brass metal craft.

Though not as beautiful as the bronze figures, **Wooden Carvings** in deodar and sheesham wood hold a special place in the hearts of Chamba's rural folk. This tradition dates to the 8th century AD, and follows a strict iconography for carved images making gods and goddesses easily identifiable by their features, decorations, and weaponry. The emphasis is on the perpetuation of religious beliefs and not aesthetic beauty,

◀ Left: Traditional articles used in prayer across India

though they do retain a certain unsophisticated charm – myths, legends and folklore are carried unchanged down generations in these carvings.

More attractive for those looking for artistic elegance are the wooden panels in classical fashion of the post-Gupta era. Superb wooden reliefs with a strong Pahari miniature influence adorn many temples – smaller carvings on the temple pillars and larger ones in the verandah. These panels illustrate everyday activities as well as religious rituals. The figures, even when not finely detailed, blend to create a harmonious whole. Also fascinating are the wooden masks of Chamba, especially Chhatrari, which are among the best in the state. Chamba is also home to a stunning array of other woodcarvings, a wide variety of toys, bowls, and small well-crafted figurines absolutely unique to the district.

Nearly as famous as the Chamba *rumaal*, the region's **Chappals** have been part of hill life for centuries. The story goes that a Chamba king designed his own slippers because he found the available variety heavy and uncomfortable. The slippers thus born were not only more comfortable, they were also considerably lighter – ideal for trekking and hiking when combined with woollen socks.

These flat, open-toed sandals in sheep and goat leather, as well as calf skin, with partially woven vamps, are available today in plain and embroidered varieties. Often, untwisted raw silk yarn and gold threads called *russi-tilla* are embroidered on to velvet. The embellished velvet is then pasted on the upper part of leather sandals. In keeping with the times, designs with characteristic lantana flowers have now been adapted for belts and fancy shoes.

▼ Below: A display of Chamba slippers

Another craft widely practiced in the hill regions of India is **Basket-weaving**. Baskets of various shapes and sizes are traditionally made by the Dumanas, a community that has been in the trade for centuries. Apart from conical baskets called *kiltu*, made for the daily use of farmers, these Dumanas also turn out handy bowls, trays and other containers with elegant handles, cushions, seats locally known as *binnas*, and mats (*chatais*) as well as cages (*pinjra*) and charming umbrellas called *chhatroru*. Basket weavers use a short, fine grass called *niru*, as well as seed willow branches and bamboo grass to make exquisite products using the method of coiling, followed by intertwining and interlacing. All rural women know some form of basket-weaving and work together while exchanging snatches of song.

Pottery is another craft, primarily the occupation of the Kumhar caste, who usually turn out articles of daily use like pitchers and pots, earthen lamps and toys, some of which are painted over with floral designs and bought by tourists for decorative purposes.

A more visible and intriguing craft however is **Jewellery**, which is often displayed in abundance on women, especially on those from tribal communities. Women wear a variety of necklaces such as *dod-malas*, *jo-malas*, *kapoor-malas*, *galpattus*, *kachs*, *hanslis* and *chandrahars* to adorn their necks; *karanphuls* and *jhumkas* on their ears; silver hair

clips, nose rings and studs, and charming anklets and bangles.

The caste of goldsmiths, locally known as Suniars, produces these ornaments in gold and more commonly in silver. Silver jewellery with deep blue and green enamelling is the particular favourite of local women. Depending on their tribe, the women of Chamba wear different jewellery: Gaddi women wear all the above, as well as the *champakali haar* and the religious *sabi* necklace with a locket containing painted images of Shiva-Parvati. Churah women wear coral necklaces in addition to those named above, in gold and silver; and the women of Pangi do not wear any jewellery whatsoever on their heads and feet. The introduction of jewellery into Chamba cannot be accurately dated, but from the 7th century onwards there are paintings, wooden and metal sculptures sporting ornamentation.

Excellent examples of all the crafts described so far can be seen at the Bhuri Singh Museum in Chamba town. These crafts are also highlighted during the annual Minjar fair, held every August in the Chaugan. Efforts to revive some of Chamba's arts and crafts are underway at the Rang Mahal in Chamba town, and these crafts are now slowly reappearing into the limelight they so justly deserve.

▲ Above: A model of a bride from Pangi in traditional attire

▼ Below: A lovely silver necklace from Chamba

▼ Below left: In Chamba town, enthusiastic shoppers buy jewellery in the bazaar

BHURI SINGH MUSEUM

In the early years of the 20th century Chamba, with its varied archaeological treasures, majestic monuments and pristine sculptures attracted the attention of J. Ph. Vogel – a respected Indologist who made extensive explorations of the area, amassing a wealth of inscriptions, engraved both on metal and stone, greatly significant to the region's history. With these discoveries, it became imperative to protect the finds from unfavourable climatic conditions and vandalism.

▲ Above: Detail from a painting depicts Krishna with a ball of butter. Dated 1740 AD

◀ Left: An old photograph of Chamba captures the bustle of the town

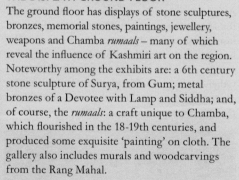

Above: Raja Bhuri Singh

When Vogel took this matter to Chamba's ruler Raja Bhuri Singh, the enlightened king transferred the epigraphic collection and other relics of the past, along with his own private collection of art, to a public building close to the Chaugan.

Eventually, on 14 September 1908, the Bhuri Singh Museum opened its doors to the public. Since then, this institution has preserved the district's cultural and artistic heritage and attempted to spread knowledge of Chamba's past to the people through various activities and programmes. The present building was constructed by the State Government to replace the old building because many antiquities and art objects were added to the collection through explorations, gifts and purchase, and a need was felt to set up more galleries. The renovated Museum opened for the second time in 1985.

Today, the Museum has over 5,000 examples of Art, Archaeology, Craft and Cultural Anthropology in its collection – mainly from Chamba district, but also some from other parts of the country.

THE DISPLAY: GROUND FLOOR

The ground floor has displays of stone sculptures, bronzes, memorial stones, paintings, jewellery, weapons and Chamba *rumaals* – many of which reveal the influence of Kashmiri art on the region. Noteworthy among the exhibits are: a 6th century stone sculpture of Surya, from Gum; metal bronzes of a Devotee with Lamp and Siddha; and, of course, the *rumaals*: a craft unique to Chamba, which flourished in the 18-19th centuries, and produced some exquisite 'painting' on cloth. The gallery also includes murals and woodcarvings from the Rang Mahal.

Above: J. Ph. Vogel

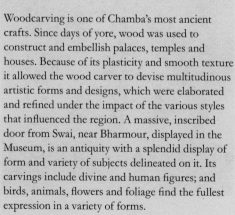

Woodcarving is one of Chamba's most ancient crafts. Since days of yore, wood was used to construct and embellish palaces, temples and houses. Because of its plasticity and smooth texture it allowed the wood carver to devise multitudinous artistic forms and designs, which were elaborated and refined under the impact of the various styles that influenced the region. A massive, inscribed door from Swai, near Bharmour, displayed in the Museum, is an antiquity with a splendid display of form and variety of subjects delineated on it. Its carvings include divine and human figures; and birds, animals, flowers and foliage find the fullest expression in a variety of forms.

◀ Left: A beautiful image of Rama

Also on the ground floor, the archaeological gallery displays stone sculptures, memorial stones and terracotta figures. Chamba's memorial stones, unique in Indian art, are usually decorated with motifs such as lotus roundels, creepers, striding elephants, horse-riders, soldiers, Varuna, Shiva *lingas*, Ganga and Yamuna. Many are carved in Takri and Sharda scripts.

▲ Above: A stone image of Vishnu in the Vaikuntha style, dated to the 17th century

Also known as *panihara*, fountain stones are found near water springs. These slabs and their inscriptions record the stories of their times and have proved invaluable to historians.

Other displays include sculptures from other districts of Himachal Pradesh as well as artefacts from the Shunga, Kushana and Gupta periods.

◀ Left: A beautiful *rumaal* depicts the *Ragamandala*

THE DISPLAY: FIRST FLOOR

The Museum's first floor houses a fascinating numismatic collection, as well as Pahari paintings and epigraphic records.

The miniature paintings of the hill states are a treasure. They differ from Mughal works in their simplicity and freshness, and from Rajasthani paintings in their lyricism. Most of the best work was produced between the 17th-19th centuries and includes the brilliantly coloured and animated Basohli paintings; the naturalistic Guler paintings, with their slender, delicately painted female figures; and the rhythmic lines and graceful women of Kangra paintings. Many works use themes from the epics, *Puranas*, *Gita-Govinda* and other poetry.

The epigraphic section, meanwhile, includes inscriptions on metal and stone, and covers the history of almost 1,000 years. Most inscriptions record the grant of land and the formation of treaties, and are preserved on copper plates. The same gallery also has some important Takri and Persian paper documents, which record the relations between Chamba's kings and the Mughals and Durranis.

Finally, the collection of coins, dating as far back as the ancient punchmarks, Kuninda, Indo-Greek and Gupta coins, and including Mughal coins as well as local issues, form a fascinating historical record. A more contemporary record exists in the form of old photographs of Chamba town, which complete the tour of the Bhuri Singh Museum.

▼ Below: A late 18th century painting shows Brahma and other deities paying homage to Vishnu

FESTIVALS OF CHAMBA

Chaitra
(March-April)

Sui Mata Mela is held in commemoration of Raja Sahila Varman's queen, who sacrificed her life for the welfare of her people, and celebrated exclusively by women. *(See p. 56)*.

Vaishaka
(April-May)

Baisakhi, also known as Bisoa, marks a successful harvest and the beginning of a new year. Rituals include distributing grain and fruit to Brahmins in the name of family ancestors, and celebratory feasting.

Jyaistha
(May-June)

Nag Panchami involves praying to Nag Devta. Images of snakes are made in houses, usually by men, and are then worshipped.

Shravana
(July-August)

Minjar Mela *(see p. 62-63)*.

Bhadrapada
(August-September)

Manimahesh Yatra is an annual pilgrimage held in honour of Shiva. Pilgrims journey to the Manimahesh lake, at the base of the peak which is considered one of the god's mountain abodes. It is interesting that no one has ever scaled this peak – according to legend, a Gaddi shepherd who attempted the feat with his flock was turned to stone. (See p. 42-43).

Asvina
(September-October)

Phul Yatra is held over four days in Pangi and is the last festival before winter sets in, so it is celebrated with special vigour and joy. Song and dance are its highlights.

Rath Rathni coincides with the rise of the new moon and is held in Chamba town. Participants create a *rath*, or wooden square tied with cloth, at the Hari Rai temple; and a *rathni*, or model of a woman, at the Lakshmi-Narayana complex. Both meet at the Chaugan, after which the *rathni* is taken to Champavati, while the *rath* is paraded across town before being returned to the Chaugan and taken apart.

Kartika (October-November)	Diwali is celebrated across India with the lighting of lamps, worship of Lakshmi and distribution of sweets.
Magha (January-February)	Khaul Mela is celebrated in Pangi, with processions at night, in the light of the full moon. A lit lamp is taken to local deities. Later, there is feasting and more torches are lit. These are flung at trees, and it is held that he whose torch gets caught in the branches will have a son.
Phalguna (February-March)	Sheel Mela marks the return of spring to Pangi. It involves worshipping Lakshmi and visiting relatives, with gifts of *sattu* and wheatcakes.

Sources: Chamba: The Official Government Website and
The Encyclopaedic District Gazetteers of India, Vol. III (S. C Bhatt (ed.), 1977)

Chamba District Factfile

Area in Sq. kms	6,522
Density per Sq. km	71
Number of statutory towns	5
Number of inhabited villages	1,118
Number of households	87,029
Total population	4,60,887
Literacy status	62.9%

Source: Census of India 2001

ACCESS AND CLIMATE

The best way of travelling to Chamba from Delhi is to take a train to Pathankot or Chakki Bank, in Punjab, and then travel by road, either by taxi or bus, both of which are easily available. There are several road connections between Chamba and Shimla, though the one via Chandigarh and Pathankot is the most popular for tourists. Dalhousie is at a distance of about 80 kms from Pathankot. Being a hill-station, Dalhousie rarely experiences very warm weather – even in summers the evenings can get chilly, though the sun is bright and strong all day.

From Dalhousie, there are two roads to Chamba town. One goes via Khajjiar and is slightly shorter (about 45 kms), while the other bypasses Khajjiar and is along the Ravi river. This second route is slightly longer at about 55 kms. The district capital at Chamba is warmer than Dalhousie, though even here temperatures can dip to 0°C in winters. Summers last from April to July, when the weather is pleasant, and maximum temperatures go up to 38°C. From July to September is the monsoon, when it is not advisable to travel through the hills, as roads become slippery and landslides can occur. However, the weather gets dry again in late September and October. Bharmour, about 65 kms from Chamba town, has similar weather though, at over 2,100 m, it is much colder.

A visit to Pangi, however, requires very detailed planning. Those coming from Chamba town must cross the Sach pass, over 4,000 m high, and the pass is only open during the peak of summer. A somewhat easier, motorable road goes via Lahaul to Pangi's administrative headquarters in Killar. though this too is a fair weather road open only between July and late September. Another fair weather road is from Kistwar in Jammu and Kashmir, though militant activity in that region tends to discourage visitors from taking this option. There are periodic helicopter flights to Pangi, but it is difficult to determine schedules of flights too much in advance.

HISTORICAL MONUMENTS OF HIMACHAL PRADESH

Himachal Pradesh is known for its extraordinary architectural heritage that has been preserved through the ages. It is also known for its sheer abundance of temples, many of which are important pilgrimage sites. Below is a partial list of these temples as well as the state's Buddhist monasteries, stupas and forts:

Bilaspur

Bilaspur	Lakshmi-Naryana Temple
Dhollera	Baba Nahar Singh Temple
Diara	Hanuman Temple
Makri	Markandei Temple
Naina Devi	Naina Devi

Hamirpur

Sarli	Gurna Jhari Temple
	Shani Dev Temple
Shah Talai	Baba Balak Nath Temple
	Vat Vriksha Temple

Kangra

Ashapuri	Ashapuri Temple
Baijnath	Baijnath Temple
	Mahakal Temple
	Mukat Nath Temple

	Shiva Temple
	Siddhanath Temple
Chaitru	Bhim ka Tila (Buddhist Stupa)
Chamunda Dham	Chamunda
	Nandikeshwar Temple
Damtal	Damtal Temple
Dharamshala	Bhagsu Nag Temple
	Darveshwar Mahadev Temple
	Lord Elgin's Tomb
Jwalamukhi	Ashtabhuja Mata Temple
	Jwalamukhi Temple
Kangra	Brajeshwari Devi Temple
	Kangra Fort
Khanihara	Rock inscription
Kotla	Kotla Fort
Masrur	Masrur Rock Cut Temples
Nagrota Surian	Badri Vishal Temple
	Narsingh Temple

Bhimakali Temple

Nurpur	Nurpur Fort	Panchavaktra Temple
Pathiyar	Rock inscription	Trilokinath Temple
Tira Sujanpur	Katoch Palace	*Mangarh* — Shiva Temple
	Narbadeshwar Temple	

Kinnaur

Nako	Nako Monastery
Pooh	Pooh Monastery

Shimla

Dattnagar	Dattatreya Temple
Hatkoti	Hateshwari Mata Temple
Rampur	Ajodya Nath Temple
	Durga Temple
Shimla	Hanuman Temple (on Jakhoo Hill)
	Sankat Mochan Temple
	Tara Devi Temple
	Vice-Regal Lodge
Sarahan	Bhimakali Temple
Sarahan (Chopal)	Bijat Devta Temple

Kullu

Bajaura	Basheshwar Mahadeva
Dassal	Gauri Shankar Temple
Jagatsukh	Shiva Temple
Manali	Hadimba Devi Temple
Naggar	Gauri Shankar Temple

Lahaul-Spiti

Dhankar	Dhankar Fort and Monastery
Kaza	Kye Monastery
Keylong	Guru Ghantal Monastery
Tabo	Tabo Monastery
Udaipur	Mrikula Devi Temple
	Trilokinath Temple

Sirmour

Paonta Sahib	Paonta Sahib Gurdwara
Thakur	Dwaradei Sahib Temple
Trilokpur	Balasundari Devi Temple

Mandi

Mandi	Ardhanarishwar Temple
	Barsela Monuments

Solan

Solan	Shulini Devi Temple

Una

Chintpurni	Chintpurni Temple

Source: List of Centrally Protected Monuments of Himachal Pradesh (Archaeological Survey of India) and List of Temples included in Schedule I of the Himachal Pradesh Hindu Public Religious Institute and Charitable Endowments Act (1984)

Baijnath Temple

BIBLIOGRAPHY

Bhatt, S. C. (ed.) *The Encyclopaedic District Gazetteers of India* (New Delhi, 1997)

Chaudhari, Minakshi *Exploring Pangi Himalaya: A World Beyond Civilisation* (New Delhi, 1998)

Dubey, Manjulika and Toby Sinclair (eds.) *Insight Guides Western Himalaya* (Singapore, 1992)

Eliade, Mircea *The Encyclopaedia of Religion* (New York, 1987)

Erndl, Kathleen M. *Victory to the Mother: The Hindu Goddess of Northwest India in Myth, Ritual and Symbol* (New York, 1993)

Gazetteer of the Chamba State: 1904 (Reprint: New Delhi, 1996)

Goetz, Hermann *The Early Wooden Temples of Chamba* (The Netherlands, 1955)

Harle, J. C. *The Art and Architecture of the Indian Subcontinent* (Yale, 1994)

Himachal Tourism, *India: A Himalayan Experience* (New Delhi)

Kamiya, Takeo *Architecture of the Indian Subcontinent* (Tokyo, 1996)

Nagar, S. L. *The Temples of Himachal Pradesh* (New Delhi, 1990)

Ohri, Vishwa Chander (ed.) *Arts of Himachal* (Shimla, 1975)

Postel, M, A. Neven and K. Mankodi *Antiquities of Himachal* (Mumbai, 1985)

Shashi, S. S. *Himachal: Nature's Peaceful Paradise* (Delhi, 1971)

Singh, K. N. *People of India Vol. XXIV: Himachal Pradesh* (Delhi, 1996)

Thakur, Laxman S. *The Architectural Heritage of Himachal Pradesh: Origin and Development of Temple Styles* (New Delhi, 1996)

Thakur, M. R. *Myths, Rituals and Beliefs in Himachal Pradesh* (New Delhi, 1997)

Verma, V. *Pangi: A Tribal Habitat in Mid-Himalaya* (Delhi, 1998)

Vogel, J. Ph. *Antiquities of Chamba* (New Delhi, 1994)

Inside Shulini Devi Temple

INDEX